Crafts for Baby

Crafts for Baby

BEAUTIFUL GIFTS AND PRACTICAL PROJECTS

Alison Jenkins

This is a Parragon Publishing Book

First published in 2007

Parragon Publishing

Queen Street House

4 Queen Street

Bath BA1 1HE, UK

Copyright © Parragon Books Ltd 2007

All rights reserved. No part of this publication may be

reproduced, stored in a retrieval system, or transmitted,

in any form or by any means, electronic, photocopying,

recording, or otherwise, without the prior permission of

the copyright holder.

ISBN: 978-1-4054-8645-3

Printed in China

CREATED AND PRODUCED BY THE BRIDGEWATER BOOK COMPANY LTD

PHOTOGRAPHY: *Simon Punter*

STYLIST: *Isabel de Cordova*

MODELS: *Tabitha Kitch, Finlay Warner, and Kazuo Williams*

Contents

Introduction

Getting started

A new baby—what a joy! Everyone looks forward to the arrival of a new member of the family, but for a new parent those anxious months before the birth can seem like a lifetime. During pregnancy, the "nesting" instinct is extremely strong. Apart from the obvious task of preparing the nursery for the new baby, you may find yourself compulsively reorganizing the kitchen cupboards or rearranging the furniture. This book shows you how to put your excess energies to a more productive and creative use. Try to make the most of this time because when the baby arrives there won't be enough hours in the day.

crafts for baby

★ The four sections of this book contain 32 step-by-step projects to make gifts that range from practical to decorative, from clothes to toys. Some are very simple indeed, such as the lampshade or mobile, and will take only an hour or two to complete. Others, like the beautiful crib quilt, require a little more time and effort.

You may want to create items for your own baby or perhaps make a thoughtful token or useful gift for a friend or relative. A handmade present will always be special because of the thought and time that you put into choosing and making the gift. A present made by hand is personal, unique, individual, and, above all, made with love —and that is priceless.

These projects cover a range of crafts and skills from sewing to woodwork—but don't worry, you don't have to be an expert craftsperson. All you need to do is follow a few simple directions. Take your time. You could be making a future family heirloom to be treasured by your children, and perhaps for generations to come.

basic equipment

★ Most of the projects described in this book require little or no specialty equipment in order to make them. If you are interested in crafts, you may already have all the basic sewing and painting items required. Take a look at the lists in the boxes opposite to give you an idea of what you might need; only two projects require power tools other than a domestic sewing machine and a steam iron. If you do not have these (an electric drill and a jigsaw), it will be simpler and cheaper to just borrow them from a friend rather than to buy them. Equipment specific to each project is listed under "materials." Always check the list first and make sure you have everything you need before you begin.

POWER EQUIPMENT

★ sewing machine
★ electric drill plus assorted bits and countersinking bit
★ jigsaw plus straight cutting and scrolling blades
★ steam iron

MISCELLANEOUS MATERIALS

★ fabrics
★ felt
★ Wonder-Under™
★ iron-on interfacing
★ craft foam
★ ribbons
★ cords
★ patternmaking paper
★ tracing paper
★ stencil acetate
★ thick card
★ latex paint
★ acrylic paint
★ clear acrylic varnish
★ wood filler

SEWING KIT

★ fabric-cutting scissors
★ small embroidery scissors
★ paper scissors
★ scalpel
★ tailor's chalk
★ sewing and embroidery needles
★ pins
★ bodkin
★ safety pin
★ sewing threads
★ embroidery threads
★ tape measure
★ rule

ADHESIVES

★ double-sided adhesive tape
★ painter's tape
★ low tack painter's tape
★ spray stencil adhesive
★ tacky craft glue
★ wood glue
★ fabric adhesive

DECORATIVE AND CONSTRUCTIVE EQUIPMENT

★ pencil
★ rule
★ screwdriver
★ staple gun
★ hole punch
★ paintbrushes
★ artist's paintbrushes
★ stencil brushes
★ junior hacksaw
★ filling knife
★ long-nose pliers

SAFETY NOTE

Sharp instruments, power tools, paints, adhesives, or any other crafter's material or equipment that is likely to be harmful to babies or small children should always be used and stored safely and carefully— and well out of the reach of curious little hands! Always check that all needles and sharp tools are removed from the product before giving it to a child.

preparation

★ All 32 projects are clearly explained in six steps and most have pattern templates or diagrams you can trace or copy. You will them find at the end of the book. Some of the patterns will need to be enlarged on a photocopier. All the patterns and templates have cutting and color/fabric indications to help you. All fabric measurements are based on using material of a minimum width of 60 in (152 cm). Always copy design, guide, or construction lines carefully onto your patterns before cutting out your material. Colors and materials used in the projects are designed to be a guide. Feel free to choose your own combinations.

Basic sewing skills

seams

PLAIN SEAM

★ Plain seams are used throughout this book where it is necessary to join two pieces of fabric together. Small projects can be hand stitched, but we advise you to use a sewing machine for speed and effectiveness. Most projects list the seam allowance to be used. Where it is not specified the seam should be ⅝ in (1.5 cm).

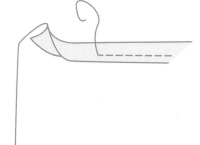

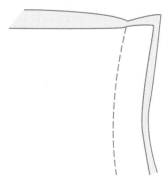

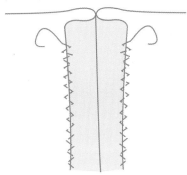

1 Place the fabrics with the right sides together. Pin or baste the seam securely, then stitch ⅝ in (1.5 cm) from the raw edge.

2 Neaten the raw edges as directed, but otherwise use a zigzag machine stitch if necessary, and then press the seam open using a steam iron.

hems

★ A hem is a double fold along the edge of a fabric piece, used to neaten a raw edge. Measure and fold the hem according to the measurements given, then stitch close to the first folded edge.

1 Fold once along the raw edge and pin or baste in place, then fold a second time to enclose the raw edge.

2 Stitch close to the first fold.

casings

★ A casing is a channel stitched through two layers of fabric to take a drawstring or piece of elastic. Casings can either run along the edge of the fabric and look like a hem or be positioned a little way down from the edge, to give a short, frilled effect above the casing.

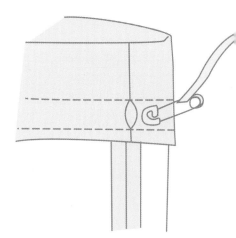

1 This casing is simply a double hem, secured with a single line of stitching along the edge of the fabric.

2 The second casing is made by working a double line of stitching positioned a little way down from the edge of the fabric. You will see that the initial hem is wider and can be a single fold of fabric.

3 Once the casing is stitched, unpick a few stitches in the seam that lies across the casing. Attach a safety pin to the end of the elastic or drawstring and thread it through the casing.

gathering

★ Gathering stitches are used to reduce the width of a large piece of fabric so that it fits a smaller one, usually to create shaping or as a design feature.

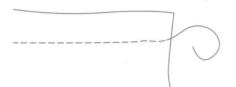 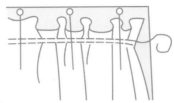

① Work a row of hand running stitches across the area to be gathered, or use the largest sewing machine straight stitch. Secure one end and leave the other long.

② Pull the gathering thread so that the fabric draws together. When it is the correct size, pin or baste and then stitch to the smaller piece, matching the raw edges.

curves, corners, and points

★ When making fabric shapes, it is often necessary to turn the item through to the right side. If the shape has corners, points, or curved seams, you need to trim or clip the seam allowance so that the fabric lies flat and neat on the right side.

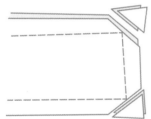 

① For a corner or sharp point, snip diagonally across the seam allowance before turning the item—this reduces the thickness of the seam allowance inside.

② For a curved seam, clip out little "v" shapes at intervals along the raw edge, so that the seam allowance will lie flat on the inside.

bias binding

★ Bias bindings are a neat and decorative way of finishing a raw edge, and especially useful if the edge is a tight or small curve where a normal hem would be difficult to fold.

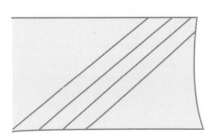 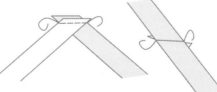

① Bias strips are cut in parallel diagonal lines across the fabric. For most projects, the strips are 1½ in (4 cm) wide.

② The strips are combined to make one piece. Place the strips with right sides together matching the diagonal edge, then machine stitch, taking a ¼ in (6 mm) seam allowance. Press the seam open.

topstitching

★ After a shape or item is complete or has been turned through to the right side and pressed, topstitching can be used as a decorative detail or to keep the finished seam flat. Simply machine stitch close to the edge of the double fabric once, or sometimes twice. You can use matching sewing thread or a contrasting color.

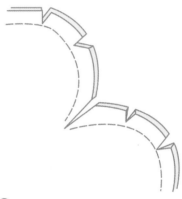

③ For an internal corner—on heart or flower shapes for example—you must clip right into the seam allowance to the stitching line, as shown.

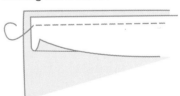

③ Working from the right side, stitch the binding along the raw edge of the fabric with right sides together. Fold a narrow hem along the remaining raw edge.

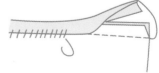

④ On the wrong side, wrap the binding around the raw edge and slipstitch the fold to the original stitching line.

Surface decoration

embroidery stitches

★ Simple embroidery stitches are used throughout the book to neaten raw edges and add decorative touches and details. The following diagrams show how to do cross-stitch, blanket stitch, running stitch, backstitch, and satin stitch.

BLANKET STITCH

CROSS-STITCH

BACKSTITCH

SATIN STITCH

RUNNING STITCH

appliqué

★ Appliqué is the name given to the application of a decorative fabric shape to another fabric. This can be done by hand or machine.

MACHINE APPLIQUÉ

❶ Machine appliqué makes use of a clever double-sided adhesive material called Wonder-Under™. First trace your shape onto the paper side of a piece of Wonder-Under™, then iron it to the wrong side of the fabric to be appliquéd.

❷ Cut out the shape carefully, then peel away the Wonder-Under™ backing paper.

❸ Use a warm iron to fuse the cut-out shape to the base fabric, then use a small machine zigzag stitch around the edge of the shape to secure.

HAND APPLIQUÉ

❶ Cut out the shape to be applied (most templates have a ¼-in/6-mm seam allowance included), then baste in position on the base fabric.

❷ Using the tip of your needle, tuck the raw edge under the shape, then slipstitch the resulting fold to the base fabric.

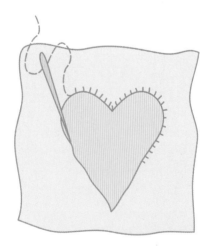

Woodworking

stenciling

⭐ Using a stencil is an extremely quick and easy method of applying repeated motifs in paint, to fabric or any other flat surface. Simply trace the stencil design onto paper, then fix the paper to a sheet of thick card. Tape a sheet of clear acetate film over the design, then, on a safe cutting surface, carefully cut out the shapes, following the pencil lines and using a scalpel or sharp craft knife. Remove the stencil and apply some spray stencil adhesive to the back. Place the stencil in position on the fabric. Pour some acrylic paint onto a saucer or palette, then take up a little paint on the bristles of a stencil brush. Wipe away the excess paint on a piece of paper towel, then apply the paint to the fabric through the stencil using a dabbing motion. Several colors can be used on the same stencil, but you must use a different brush for each color.

power tools

⭐ Using power tools can be a little daunting but they are quite safe when used correctly. Be sure to wear a protective mask when drilling or cutting, as these tools create a lot of dust.

USING A JIGSAW

Use a power jigsaw for making cuts in sheet materials such as plywood. Begin by placing your material on a workbench, then hold the jigsaw firmly and start the motor. Slowly guide the blade along the cutting line. Always work slowly and carefully. Use a straight cutting blade for straight cuts and a scrolling blade for curves.

USING A DRILL

An electric drill makes light work of hole-making in all sorts of materials—simply use the correct diameter bit to match the hole required. Always make sure that the drill bit is inserted into the drill correctly and keep the drill straight.

pilot holes and countersinking

Before inserting a screw into a piece of wood, you must first make a "pilot hole." This is a drilled hole a little smaller than the diameter of the screw itself. The pilot hole acts as a guide for the screw and prevents the wood splitting. The pilot hole may then be "countersunk" using a countersinking drill bit. This makes a shallow recess at the entrance to the pilot hole so the screw head can lie flush with the surrounding surface. You can hide the hole with wood filler and paint.

gluing

Wood and plywood should always be joined using wood glue—it dries to make an extremely strong bond. Apply a bead of glue to the surfaces to be joined and then press both together firmly. Wipe away any excess glue that may seep out from the join using a damp cloth, then let the join dry.

preparing plywood for painting

Plywood is a versatile material made from thin layers of wood compressed together to make a thick sheet. When plywood is cut, gaps or "voids" are sometimes seen along the cut edge. These are simply air gaps between the layers, but they must be repaired with a wood filler before painting. Apply the filler using a filling knife, smoothing out the surface with the blade. When the filler is dry, use sandpaper to rub the repaired area smooth. This filling method can also be used to repair any surface damage.

painting

Painting is a relatively easy job, but to get the best results always rely on adequate preparation beforehand. When applying paint onto a bare wood, plywood, or MDF surface, a suitable primer must be applied first. This prepares the surface and creates a good key for the topcoat. Let the primer dry completely before applying the topcoat, and if necessary sand down the primed surface and apply a second coat. Remember to wipe away all dust particles using a damp cloth after sanding.

For the nursery

Crib quilt

What better way to spend those last weeks before your baby arrives than making a traditional quilt? The larger pieces are machine stitched together, but the heart motifs and general quilting are done by hand. Spend time and care over the hand stitching to make this quilt an item that will last a lifetime.

materials

- pencil and tracing paper
- sewing kit (see page 9) and sewing machine
- 8 in (20 cm) each of 6 or more red and white gingham, striped, spotted, and patterned fabrics
- 20 in (50 cm) plain red fabric
- 4 in (10 cm) white and red polka dot fabric
- 39½ in (1 m) lightweight wadding
- 39½ in (1 m) red gingham fabric for backing
- steam iron

NOTE *When choosing your fabrics, try to include three light-toned and three darker-toned patterns that work well together and with plain white and red. All templates include a ¼-in (6-mm) seam allowance.*

TEMPLATES P87

① Trace the heart motif, strap (the rectangular strip between the large squares), and corner square templates provided on page 87 onto tracing paper. You will also need a pattern for the large square patches, which are simply 7-in (17.5-cm) squares.

② To begin, you need to cut out the following:
- 12 large squares: 6 light-toned pattern and 6 dark-toned red and white patterned or striped fabric
- 12 heart-shaped motifs: 6 light-toned pattern and 6 dark-toned fabrics
- 17 rectangular straps from plain red fabric
- 10 corner squares from red polka dot fabric (try to keep a dot in the center of the square)
- approximately 158 in (4 m) of 1½-in (4-cm) wide bias strips from plain red fabric
- approximately 158 in (4 m) of 1½-in (4-cm) wide straight strips from red and white striped fabric
- 39½-in x 29½-in (1-m x 75-cm) rectangle of polyester wadding
- 39½-in x 29½-in (1-m x 75-cm) rectangle of red gingham for backing

③ Take the large squares and the heart shapes and experiment with different pattern combinations—you will find that some work better than others. When you are satisfied, baste each heart into position about ⅝ in (1.5 cm) from the raw edge. Turn the raw edge of the fabric heart to the wrong side using the tip of

your needle and slipstitch the fold in place neatly. (See hand appliqué, step 2 on page 12.)

④ Lay the large squares on the floor, 4 x 3 squares to make a rectangle, alternating light and dark shades. Place a red strap between each square and along the outside edges. Now place a small square at each corner. Stitch all the pieces together one row at a time taking a ¼ in (6 mm) seam allowance, then stitch the rows together to make the quilt top. This may take a little while, but it is worth taking time to make sure that all the corners are neat and matching. Press the seams open at each stage.

⑤ Stitch a red-and-white striped strip to each long side of the quilt top first, then across the short ends. Now sandwich the wadding between the quilt top and the gingham backing fabric. Baste the three layers together vertically and horizontally at approximately 4-in (10-cm) intervals. Now work a small running stitch through all the layers along the main seam lines. Try to keep the stitches small and regular, and wear a thimble to save your fingertip!

⑥ When the quilting is complete, remove all basting stitches and trim the edge of the quilt top neatly. Join the plain red bias strips together to form one continuous length, then apply the binding to the outside edge (see page 11). To make this easier, trim the corners of the quilt to a softly rounded shape before binding.

Lampshade

This is a very simple decorative project that can be completed in an hour or two, with an underwater marine theme that is calm and soothing. However, you could adapt the idea to make a brighter shade using other colors. You can also use it as a pendant shade; the soft shadows cast around the nursery will hopefully capture your tiny baby's attention.

materials

- pencil and tracing paper
- scissors
- tape measure
- pale blue drum-shaped lampshade (plus base if required)
- large pale blue polypropylene sheet
- white craft foam sheet
- hole punch
- double-sided adhesive pads
- double-sided adhesive tape

TEMPLATES P88

① To begin, trace the wave and fish templates provided on page 88 onto tracing paper, then cut out carefully. Indicate the eye position on each fish shape with a small circle or pencil dot.

② Measure the exact circumference of your shade, then add approximately ¾ in (2 cm) for an overlap. Extend the wave shape to make a new template that matches this measurement.

③ Lay the wave template onto the polypropylene sheet and trace around the edge using a sharp pencil. Repeat this to make two wave strips, but you can use more if your shade is larger. Now cut along the pencil lines carefully using scissors.

④ Cut out small and large fish shapes from the white craft foam sheet in the same way. The number will depend on the size of your shade, but use approximately 10 large fish and 30 smaller ones. Remember to indicate the eye on each fish, then make a small hole using the hole punch at that point.

⑤ Take the double-sided adhesive pads and fix three or four at equally spaced intervals on one side of each wave. Peel off the backing paper and fix around the shade. Use a tab of double-sided adhesive tape to secure the overlap. Do likewise with the other or subsequent strips.

⑥ Stick an adhesive pad to the back of each fish shape. You may trim the pad to fit if it is too large for the small shapes. Fix the fish to the waves, alternating large and groups of small shapes.

Wirework initials

These delicate wirework initials make a thoughtful gift for friends to mark the arrival of their new baby, and can easily be sent through the mail as a greeting. However, you could make the gift a little more special by making a drawstring bag and gift box to hold it. Copy the heart-shaped template first, then practice drawing a nice cursive initial in the center. Alternatively, you could make a decorative pattern instead of an initial if you prefer.

materials

- pencil and tracing paper
- painter's tape
- piece of stiff card
- ¹/₁₆-in (2-mm) diameter colored craft wire
- long-nose pliers
- fine jewelry wire
- 27¹/₂ in (70 cm) pink organza ribbon for the gift pouch
- 8-in x 16-in (20-cm x 40-cm) strip white organza
- sewing kit (see page 9) and sewing machine
- steam iron
- safety pin
- 20 in (50 cm) pink organza ribbon
- gift box (optional)

⬤ TEMPLATE P88

① Trace the template provided on page 88 onto tracing paper, then enlarge to the required size. Tape the template to a piece of stiff card to use as a guide when bending the wire. The aim is to form the heart shape and wavy border from a single length of wire. It is best to practice bending and curling the wire on a short spare piece before starting the project.

② Begin with the tight scroll shape that lies at the top center of the heart, then bend the basic heart shape. Place the wire shape on the template outlines as you work to make sure the shape is correct.

③ Next, bend the small wavy border that surrounds the central shape. This is a little fiddly but will become easier as you work. Snip off the wire neatly when the shape is complete. Next, take a shorter length of wire and bend it to match the initial you have drawn. Make sure that it fits neatly inside the heart shape.

④ To keep the wires in place, they must be bound together with fine jewelry wire. Begin with the loop at the top center and work around the shape, binding each section in turn. When the heart shape is secure, place the initial in position and bind it to the frame securely.

⑤ Take the longer length of organza ribbon and tie it into a pretty bow and hanging loop around the scroll at the top of the heart shape. Trim the ends of the ribbon into neat fishtail points.

⑥ For the gift pouch, simply fold the organza strip in half, then stitch both sides together. Fold a narrow hem along the top raw edge, then fold a larger 2-in (5-cm) hem and press. Now stitch a ⁵/₈-in (1.5-cm) casing (see page 10) about 2 in (5 cm) from the top edge. Turn the pouch to the right side and press. Unpick a few stitches in the seam between the stitching lines of the casing on one side, then use a safety pin to thread the casing with ribbon. Place the wire heart inside, then gather up the pouch and tie the ribbon in a bow. Place inside a gift box if desired.

Keepsake memory box

Where do you keep all those precious tiny items that remind you of your baby's first days, months, or years? The hospital wristband, lock of baby hair, pictures of the newborn, the birth certificate, or first tiny bootees, gloves, and clothes. A memory box is the answer. The soft pastel exterior conceals a colorful fabric lining, complete with co-ordinating storage items such as a photo album, scrapbook, and note book, to record all those "firsts" and family moments that you don't want to forget.

materials

- box
- wood filler
- medium grade sandpaper
- white wood or multi-surface primer
- paintbrush
- pale yellow semigloss paint
- sewing kit (see page 9)
- 39½ in (1 m) pink fabric with a bold pattern
- steam iron
- extra tacky craft adhesive
- 118 in (3 m) white satin ribbon
- scrapbooks, photo albums, little boxes
- 20 in (50 cm) toning fabric with a smaller pattern
- double-sided adhesive tape
- staple gun

① Make sure the exterior and interior surfaces of the box are clean and dry. Repair any exterior surface imperfections with wood filler, then, when dry, rub the area down with medium grade sandpaper. Wipe away all dust particles using a damp cloth. Your box is now ready for painting.

② To ensure a good finished result, a coat of primer should be applied to bare wooden or MDF surfaces. When the primer is dry, apply two (or more if necessary) coats of semigloss paint, leaving appropriate drying time in between applications. Make sure to paint the edges of the box and lid, but leave the inside unpainted.

③ While the paint dries, cut out the pink fabric to line the interior. Cut one strip to fit around the sides, allowing for a 1-in (2.5-cm) hem at the top edge and a ⅝-in (1.5-cm) overlap at the side and lower edges, then a piece to fit the base, allowing a 1-in (2.5-cm) hem on all four sides.

④ Cut all the linings to size and fold and press the hems neatly. Apply adhesive to the sides of the box, then carefully press the lining fabric into position, matching the pressed hem to the top edge of the box and smoothing the raw edge overlap into the corners at the base. Snip into the overlap at each corner so that the fabric lies flat. Now glue the base lining into position.

⑤ The lid is lined in the same way, but stitch a pocket to the main part before gluing. Use a ribbon tie to keep the pocket closed. To accessorize the memory box, gather together a collection of scrapbooks, albums, little boxes, etc., and cover them in a coordinating fabric secured by tabs of double-sided adhesive tape. You can add to the memory box as the years go by.

⑥ Finally, cut a strip of the lining fabric approximately 2½ in x 4½ in (6 cm x 12 cm). This will form the loop with which to lift the box lid. Apply some adhesive down the center of the strip on the wrong side. Now fold both long edges to meet in the center and press firmly down onto the wet adhesive. When the adhesive is dry, fold the strip in half, then fix the end to the inside of the lid using a staple gun.

NOTE *Fabric quantities are calculated for a box approximately 12 in x 12 in x 24 in (30 cm x 30 cm x 60 cm). Allow more or less fabric for a larger or smaller box. You can use one made from plywood, solid wood, or MDF. Many craft companies produce "blank" shapes for decorative purposes, or you could use one from your own childhood, or an inexpensive "antique" from a thrift shop.*

Pocket tidy

This pretty pocket tidy with its jolly spotted fabric and colorful pockets is an ideal storage device for all those small bits and pieces required for your baby's well-being and comfort. Hang it at a suitable height so it's within easy reach when you are seated and feeding or nursing your baby.

materials

- pencil and tracing paper
- sewing kit (see page 9) and sewing machine
- 12 in (30 cm) each of four toning plain colored cotton fabrics
- 71 in (1.8 m) spotted fabric
- steam iron
- 20 in (50 cm) of 1/4-in (6-mm) wide elastic
- 2 x 39½-in (1-m) lengths of ½-in (12-mm) diameter wooden dowel
- hacksaw
- 118 in (3 m) cord

NOTE *Template and fabric measurements include a 5/8-in (1.5-cm) seam allowance.*

⬤ TEMPLATE P95

1 Trace the flap template provided on page 95 onto tracing paper, then enlarge to the size required. Now cut out the following fabric pieces:
- 2 flap pieces in each of the four plain fabrics
- 2 x 21½-in x 33½-in (55-cm x 85-cm) rectangles of spotted fabric for the base and backing
- 1 x 10½-in x 33½-in (27-cm x 85-cm) rectangle of spotted fabric for the top pockets
- 1 x 10½-in (27-cm) strip of spotted fabric across the whole width of the fabric for the lower pockets
- 1 x 4-in x 33½-in (10-cm x 85-cm) strip for the dowel channel at the lower edge
- 5 x 6-in x 3-in (15-cm x 8-cm) rectangles of spotted fabric for the hanging tabs

2 Stitch the flap pieces together in pairs around the outside edge. Trim across the seam allowance at each point (see page 11), then turn through to the right side and press. Fold and stitch a ¾-in (2-cm) double hem across one long edge of both pocket strips. Press a single ½-in (1-cm) hem at the lower edge of the shorter strip.

3 Lay the flaps side by side in a row with the points upward. Now place the hemmed edge of the shorter pocket strip on top to cover the raw edge of each flap. Pin and stitch the flaps to the strip. The flaps will fold down to cover the stitching lines. Position the pocket strip on the base rectangle 2 in (5 cm) down from the top raw edge, then stitch the pocket divisions vertically.

4 Divide the remaining strip pocket into quarters and mark the divisions with pins. Thread elastic through the hem along the top edge using a safety pin. Pull the elastic quite tight so as to gather up the central two quarters only. The gathering should correspond with the width of the middle two flap pockets. Now hand stitch through the hem and the elastic inside to secure. Pin the pocket strip in place on the backing, then pleat up the remaining fabric at each end to fit. Machine stitch the vertical pocket divisions as in step 3.

5 Fold and machine stitch a double hem down each side of the tidy and along the top edge. Take the remaining narrow fabric strip and stitch it to the lower edge with right sides facing. Fold in the seam allowance on the three raw edges, then fold the strip around the lower raw edge of the tidy, rather like a wide binding. Slipstitch the long folded edge to the backing fabric on the wrong side. Cut a length of dowel, using a hacksaw, to fit across the tidy, then insert it into the channel.

6 Fold each tab in half lengthwise with right sides facing, then stitch the long edges together taking a 5/8-in (1.5-cm) seam allowance. Turn each through to the right side and press. Fold each tab in half, then stitch the short raw edges to the wrong side of the top hem of the tidy. Slot the dowel through the tabs and tie the cord to both ends. Knot the cord securely, forming a hanging loop as shown in the picture.

Cozy blanket

A monogram or even a simple shape like a heart or a teddy can transform a plain comfort blanket into something quite special and personal. This blanket uses cream and pale blue fleece to make a reversible, double-thickness blanket. The initial is simply blanket stitched in place, cream on blue and blue on cream. Both layers are securely held together around the outside edge with a row of regular blanket stitches. You may make a blanket to fit your baby's crib, or perhaps you'd like to make a smaller one for nursing or to fit inside the stroller or Moses basket,

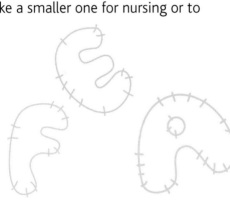

materials

- sewing kit (see page 9)
- 1 cream fleece blanket
- 1 pale blue fleece blanket
- small plate or saucer
- pencil or tailor's chalk
- plain paper
- 5 skeins cream embroidery thread
- 1 skein blue embroidery thread

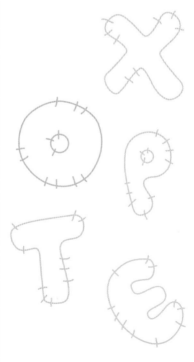

❶ First trim your fabric pieces to the size required. Place the cream fleece on top of the blue and measure carefully, and then cut through both layers at the same time. The cream layer will be trimmed a little smaller at a later stage.

❷ Use a small plate or saucer as a template to cut the corners into soft curves. Place the saucer/plate next to the right-angle corner and draw around the edge using a pencil or tailor's chalk. Cut carefully along the curved line and discard the waste.

❸ The size of the monogram depends largely on the size of the blanket. Experiment a little with a paper cut-out before you decide. For the template, draw a large letter on a piece of paper, then smooth out and round off all the sharp edges and corners to make a softly rounded squat shape. The fleece fabric is not suitable for tight curves and sharp corners.

❹ Cut out one blue and one cream letter and place each in one corner of the opposite colored fleece. Baste the letter in place, then work a neat blanket stitch using cream or blue embroidery thread around the edges (see page 12).

❺ Now place the cream fleece on top of the blue. Baste both layers together approximately 1 in (2.5 cm) from the outside edges. Using sharp scissors, trim the cream layer about ⅝ in (1.5 cm) smaller than the blue layer underneath.

❻ Fold the edge of the blue fleece over the raw edge of the cream layer to form a mock binding then tack in place. Now work a regular blanket stitch around the outside, using a cream colored embroidery thread (see page 12).

Cushions

If you love the beach, you'll adore these three cushions. The size you choose is up to you—make them tiny for a chair or larger for a day bed; simply enlarge the template as required. The basic construction and background sections are machine stitched while the smaller details are appliquéd by hand.

materials

- sewing kit (see page 9) and sewing machine
- 39½ in (1 m) blue chambray fabric for the sky and cushion backs
- 12 in (30 cm) of plain blue fabric for the sea
- steam iron
- pencil and tracing paper
- 12 in (30 cm) beige mottled pattern fabric for sand
- palm-size scraps of beige, white, red, yellow, and assorted striped fabric
- scraps of red gingham ribbon
- 3 x 20-in (50-cm) cushion pads

NOTE *Use spare scraps of fabric for small details. Each template represents the size of your cushion plus ⁵⁄₈-in (1.5 cm) seam allowance on all 4 sides.*

⬤ TEMPLATES P89

① For each cushion, cut the following pieces:
- 2 x 21-in x 13-in (53-cm x 33-cm) rectangles from blue chambray for the cushion backs
- 21-in x 11-in (53-cm x 28-cm) rectangle from blue chambray for the sky
- 21-in x 11-in (53-cm x 28-cm) rectangle from plain blue fabric for the sea

Stitch the sky and sea pieces with right sides facing, taking a ⁵⁄₈-in (1.5-cm) seam allowance, then press the seam open. This forms the background for each cushion front.

② Trace the cushion templates provided on page 89 onto tracing paper, then enlarge to the required size. You will need to retrace each of the details (beach huts, sun, sandcastles, lighthouse, boat, etc.) of the design in turn, then add a ¼-in (6-mm) seam allowance to the edges. Use the picture as a guide and cut each section in turn from the appropriate fabric.

③ Baste the "sand" in place on each of the three background squares, then turn the wavy raw edge under using the tip of your needle. Slipstitch the fold neatly to the background (see hand appliqué, step 2 on page 12). Next, appliqué the beach huts, the sun, the sandcastles, and then the basic lighthouse shape in the same way.

④ Small details like the boat and the lighthouse base and top can be tricky to apply. However, they give an extremely professional result and it is worth taking your time.

⑤ To complete the design, add some small machine-stitched details. Adjust your sewing machine to a narrow satin stitch setting and work three vertical windows down the center of the lighthouse using red thread. Trim the gingham ribbon to form two tiny pointed flags and satin stitch (see page 12) them to the sandcastles using a beige thread. Now remove all basting threads.

⑥ Fold and stitch a narrow double hem across one long edge of each of the cushion backs. Place two cushion backs onto each cushion front with right sides facing. Match the raw edges around the outside and overlap the hemmed edges in the center. Machine stitch around the outside, taking a ⁵⁄₈-in (1.5-cm) seam allowance. Trim diagonally across the seam allowance at each corner (see page 11), then turn the cushion through to the right side and press.

Elephant bookends

Yes, you are seeing pink elephants! These jolly fellows will hold a row of small books safely on a bookshelf or table top. The height of each bookend measures approximately 6 in (15 cm), but you can always enlarge the template a little more than the recommended percentage to make a bigger Jumbo for larger and heavier books—but remember you'll have to enlarge the base, too.

materials

- pencil and tracing paper
- ½-in (1-cm) thick plywood (or small offcuts from the wood yard)
- jigsaw plus blades (straight cutting blade and scrolling blade)
- medium grade sandpaper
- wood filler
- electric drill plus bits, and countersink bit
- white primer
- paintbrush
- wood glue
- 1-in (6 x 2.5-cm) long wood screws
- pink semigloss paint

TEMPLATES P87

① Trace the elephant templates provided on page 87 onto tracing paper then enlarge to the appropriate size as directed. Lay the templates on the plywood and draw around the edge using a sharp pencil. You will need two elephant shapes and four ears. Also mark out four rectangles measuring 6 in x 3 in (15 cm x 7.5 cm) for the bases.

② Place the plywood on a workbench or safe and steady cutting surface, then cut along the pencil lines with a jigsaw. Use a straight cutting blade for the base rectangles and a scrolling blade to cut the curved elephant and ear pieces.

③ You may find that the cut edges are a little splintered. If so, simply rub smooth using medium grade sandpaper. Repair any voids and surface unevenness (see painting on page 13).

④ Using a fine drill bit and an electric drill, make a small hole where indicated to represent the elephant's eye. Now apply a coat of white primer to all pieces and let dry. Examine the surfaces and sand away any unevenness. Apply a second coat of primer and resand. Wipe away all dust particles using a damp cloth in preparation for the pink topcoat.

⑤ Glue the base rectangles together to form two right angles. Let the glue set a little, then drill two pilot holes through the right-angle join. Countersink each drill hole and insert a wood screw to secure the join, then fill the screw hole and sand smooth (see page 13).

⑥ Glue the ears to each elephant and then glue the elephants' feet to each base. Let the glue dry, then screw the feet to the bases from underneath, making a pilot hole first and then countersinking the screw hole as before. Apply two coats of pink paint, letting each coat dry before applying the next.

Playroom
projects

Soft play blocks

Your baby will enjoy playing with these soft blocks on many different levels. Building, balancing, and construction will be learned at a later stage, but certainly hugging, chewing, and throwing skills will develop really quickly here. The star-shape motifs are securely held in place with double-sided adhesive material and a zigzag machine stitch.

materials

- pencil and tracing paper
- sewing kit (see page 9) and sewing machine
- 6 x 8-in (20-cm) squares in assorted pink and blue plain and patterned fabrics per block
- 8 in (20 cm) Wonder-Under™ double-sided adhesive material
- polyester toy filling

NOTE *Only the block templates include a ⅝-in (1.5-cm) seam allowance.*

● TEMPLATES P95

① Trace the templates provided on page 95 onto tracing paper, then enlarge to the appropriate size as directed. You will need six different colored fabric squares and two star shapes for each block. Use the picture as a guide to color and pattern arrangement or design your own. For cutting out the stars, see machine appliqué, page 12.

② Place your fabric pieces together in groups of six. Next, peel off the backing paper from each of the star shapes and apply to the center of two squares from each pile. Adjust your sewing machine to a narrow zigzag stitch setting and carefully stitch around the edges of each star shape.

③ To assemble each block, take the four pieces that will form the sides, then pin and machine stitch them together to form a cylinder with right sides facing, taking a seam allowance of ⅝ in (1.5 cm). Remember to leave a small gap in the stitching at the center of one of the seams so that you can turn the block to the right side.

④ Stitch the top and bottom squares to the side piece, taking care to keep the corners neat and unpuckered. You will need to snip a few stitches at each end of the side seams so that the top corners lie flat.

⑤ Turn each block through to the right side. Use your finger or the tip of a pair of scissors to gently ease out the corners from inside the shape, taking care not to burst through the seam.

⑥ Stuff each block with toy filling so it feels quite firm but not too solid—your baby should be able to grasp the block quite easily. Slipstitch the small opening in the seam using a matching sewing thread.

Mobile

A mobile is always a popular choice for a nursery—use these pretty pastel colors or choose ones to tone with the nursery color scheme. This mobile uses simple concentric circle and flower shapes that move and spin to create a focus for your little one's gaze—and probably your own! Craft foam is easy to use and cut, but colored paper or thin card would work well too. Each element of the mobile is a pair of shapes stuck together; the fine thread is sandwiched securely between the layers.

materials

- pencil and tracing paper
- scissors
- 1 x 16¹/₂-in x 11¹/₂-in (42-cm x 30-cm) piece each pink, green, and blue craft foam
- double-sided adhesive tape
- painter's tape
- beading thread
- long-nose pliers
- wire coat hanger
- yellow spray paint
- 19¹/₂ in (50 cm) yellow satin ribbon
- large needle and thread

TEMPLATES P87

① Trace the flower, circle, and disk templates provided on page 87 onto tracing paper, then enlarge to the required size as directed. Cut out the paper templates, then transfer the outlines to the colored craft foam, following the color cutting guide carefully.

② It is a good idea to set out all the larger circle, disk, and flower pieces in the appropriate pairs on your counter, using the picture as a guide to the color combinations and shape groupings. Leave a space of about 4 in (10 cm) between each flower and circle or disk group. At this stage, keep all the smallest central disks to one side.

③ When you are satisfied with your arrangement, you may begin to string the separate elements together. It's best to start with the central group. Remove the top shape of each pair, then apply strips of double-sided tape down the center of each piece. When you cut it, you will need to allow for the holes in the center of each shape. Now remove the backing papers.

④ Use a tab of painter's tape to fix the end of the beading thread to your counter about 8 in (20 cm) above the top circle. Lay the thread onto the tape, checking the length of the thread between each shape. You can now replace the top shapes, sandwiching the thread inside securely. Do likewise with the other two groups.

⑤ Use small tabs of double-sided tape to secure the small central disks to the center of each flower and circle. Using pliers, cut a 10-in (25-cm) length of wire from a coat hanger, then bend a tiny loop at each end. Apply a coat of yellow spray paint to the wire and let dry.

⑥ Place a tab of double-sided tape to the center of the ribbon length and remove the backing paper. Place the center of the wire onto the tape. Fold the ribbon around the wire and squeeze the adhesive tape together to hold the wire securely. Use a large needle to stitch the central motif group to the ribbon, then tie the other two groups to the small loop at each end of the wire. Tie the ends of the ribbon in a knot and hang the mobile in a suitable place out of reach of children.

Pull-along Patch

Woof, woof! It's easier than you think to make a cute little canine on wheels to guard your nursery and entertain a toddler. Patch's body is just a few flat plywood shapes glued together, and the wheels are actually small wooden drawer knobs fixed to short dowel axles. If you feel particularly artistic, why not paint your pulling Patch toy to match the family pet?

materials

- pencil and tracing paper
- sheet ⅝-in (1.5-cm) thick plywood
- jigsaw with scrolling blade
- medium grade sandpaper
- natural colored wood filler
- wood glue
- white primer
- paintbrush
- white semigloss paint
- black, brown, and red acrylic paints
- small artist's paintbrush
- small stencil brush
- electric drill with ¼-in (6-mm) and ⅜-in (8-mm) bits
- 4 small wooden drawer knobs
- 2 x 3-in (8-cm) lengths of ¼-in (6-mm) diameter wooden dowel
- 8 in (20 cm) red satin ribbon
- 39½ in (1 m) black satin ribbon

TEMPLATES P88

❶ Trace the body and leg templates provided on page 88 onto tracing paper, then enlarge to the size as directed. Lay the templates on the plywood and trace around the edge using a sharp pencil. You will need to cut one body, two front legs, and two hind legs. All other details are painted on later.

❷ Place the plywood on a workbench or safe and steady cutting surface, then cut along the pencil lines with a jigsaw fitted with a scrolling blade. This blade will let you cut around tight curves with ease.

❸ You may find that the cut edges are a little splintered. If so, simply rub smooth using a medium grade sandpaper. Prepare the plywood as directed on page 13.

❹ Glue the legs to the body shape and let dry completely. Next, apply a coat of white primer to both sides and edges of the shape and let dry. Examine the surfaces and sand away any unevenness. Apply a second coat of primer and resand. Wipe away all dust particles using a damp cloth in preparation for one or two coats of white semigloss paint. Apply the paint.

❺ Refer to the picture and the template design lines, then apply the eyes, ears, and dark colored patches to the dog's body with black and brown acrylic paint. Acrylic paint is the best for this type of surface decoration because it dries quickly. Paint the eyes, ears, and basic patches using a small artist's paintbrush, then soften the edges of the patches using a small stencil brush. Paint the four wooden knobs red.

❻ For the wheels, simply drill an ⅜-in (8-mm) hole through the body and leg shapes at height that will allow the bottom of the wheels to be clear of the body. Then drill a ½-in (1-cm) deep ¼-in (6-mm) diameter hole in the center of the flat underside of each wooden knob. Glue a knob to one end of each dowel and let the glue dry. Pass the dowels through the predrilled holes in the body shape, then glue on the remaining two knobs. Make a collar from the red ribbon and finally attach a black ribbon lead.

Floor mat

"Quack, quack! Croak, croak!" Jumping frogs and fluffy ducks form a pretty border to this very easy-to-make floor mat. It's just a rectangle of heavyweight natural canvas painted with leftover household latex paint—what could be simpler? Use it in the nursery, or take it out into the garden to play counting games, or to aid with storytelling in fine weather. The surface is sealed with clear varnish so any accidental spills or dirty footprints can be easily wiped away using a damp cloth.

materials

- pencil and tracing paper
- low tack painter's tape
- sheet of thick card
- sheets of stencil acetate
- scalpel
- heavyweight natural canvas
- rule
- scissors
- mini sponge roller
- white matte latex paint
- green and yellow latex paint
- spray stencil adhesive
- yellow, green, and red acrylic paint
- stencil brush
- clear satin-finish acrylic varnish
- paintbrush
- tacky craft glue

TEMPLATES P88

① Trace the frog and duck stencil templates provided on page 88 onto tracing paper, then enlarge to the appropriate size as directed. Copy each design onto a separate sheet of paper. Use tabs of painter's tape to fix the tracings to a sheet of thick card, then fix a sheet of stencil acetate over each one. Carefully cut out the stencil using a scalpel (see page 13).

② Draw and cut out a rectangle of canvas using the diagram measurements as a guide. Be sure to use a rule and measure carefully to ensure that the edges are straight and the corners true right angles. Using a mini sponge roller, apply two or three coats of white matt latex paint to the canvas, letting each coat dry before applying the next.

③ When the white paint is dry, use a rule and very faint pencil lines to indicate the border areas and colored central bands, following the measurements on the diagram. Next use long strips of low tack tape to mask off the border and central areas ready for the next painting stage.

④ Apply green and yellow latex paint to the masked-off areas using a mini sponge roller. Be sure not to overload the roller, as this may cause paint to bleed under the painter's tape. Remove all tape strips when the paint is dry.

⑤ Refer to "stenciling" on page 13 to guide you through the next stage. Make a frog stencil using green acrylic paint at each corner and at the center point of each side. Position yellow ducks on each side of the frog, reversing the stencil to make a symmetrical pattern. Remember to add a touch of red paint to accentuate the beak and webbed feet.

⑥ When all the decorative paintwork is dry, apply a coat of clear acrylic varnish to seal the surface. Leave plenty of time for the varnish to dry, then turn the mat over to the other side. Draw two pencil lines, 1 in (2.5 cm) and 5/8 in (1.5 cm) from the outer edge of the mat. Snip across each corner diagonally from the raw edge to meet the first line, then apply glue to the marked hem area. Fold over the raw edge to meet the second pencil line—making sure the corners miter neatly.

Teddy

Many adults have very fond memories of a favorite toy from childhood. Every baby deserves their very own huggable teddy bear to love, and maybe keep on loving till they grow up. This fluffy bear is filled with the softest natural fibers and is fully washable.

materials

- pencil and tracing paper
- sewing kit (see page 9) and sewing machine
- 2 in (30 cm) short pile, washable fur fabric with a brown suede underside
- natural, washable toy filling
- soft pencil or tailor's chalk
- brown embroidery thread
- ribbon for teddy's bow tie

NOTE *Patterns include a 1/4-in (6-mm) seam allowance.*

TEMPLATES PP92–93

1 Trace the teddy pattern templates provided on pages 92–93 onto tracing paper, then enlarge to the appropriate size as directed. Cut out the pattern pieces and then cut out carefully in fur fabric.

2 Fold each leg and arm piece in half with right sides facing taking a 1/4-in (6 mm) seam allowance, then stitch the long seams together. Stitch the sole pieces to the bottom of the legs, placing the reverse sides of the soles on the front of the legs. Turn each arm and leg piece to the right side and stuff with toy filling. Be sure not to overfill the pieces. Now machine stitch or baste across the opening so the filling does not spill out.

3 Take the face piece and fold in half. Stitch the long seam together (this runs from the nose to the neck). Then stitch across the short seam that will form the nose. Stitch the face to one body piece and the back of the head to the remaining body piece.

4 Place the back of the head and body flat on your counter with the right side facing you, then baste the top of each leg to the lower edge. Baste the top of each arm, then stitch the ears in place. Remember to make a small pleat in each ear piece as indicated on the pattern.

5 Fold the arms and legs inward, then place the front body and face on top. Baste the two pieces together, leaving a gap along the lower body edge so that you can turn teddy to the right side. Turn the shape through to the right side now, then stuff the body and head with toy filling. Carefully slipstitch to close the opening.

6 Using the picture as a guide, mark the eye, nose, and mouth position using a soft pencil or tailor's chalk. Thread a bodkin with brown embroidery thread, then use long satin stitches (see page 12) to make the features.

Raggedy Ann doll

Many girls adore their dolls, taking them everywhere until they become very raggedy indeed! This doll measures approximately 14 in (35 cm) in length, but you could scale the pattern up to make a larger, almost life-size doll for an older child.

materials

- pencil and tracing paper
- sewing kit (see page 9) and sewing machine
- 8 in (20 cm) white cotton fabric for head and hands
- 8 in (20 cm) pink-and-white striped cotton fabric for body and limbs
- scrap of plain pink cotton fabric for shoes
- toy filling
- broderie anglaise lace trim

- soft pencil or tailor's chalk
- blue, white, and red embroidery thread for face
- 12 in (30 cm) white cotton piqué fabric for dress
- brown chunky-weight knitting yarn for hair
- 60 in (1.5 m) pink gingham ribbon

NOTE *Templates include a ¼-in (6-mm) seam allowance aside from neck and armholes.*

🌑 TEMPLATES P92

1. Trace the doll and dress templates provided on page 92 onto tracing paper, then enlarge to the appropriate size as directed. Following the directions, cut out all the pieces from white, striped, and pink cotton fabrics. As the pieces are quite small, it is important to mark out and cut carefully and accurately.

2. With right sides together, stitch the hands to the arms and the shoes to the legs, then stitch both head and body pieces together. Fold each leg and arm piece in half with right sides facing and stitch the long seams together. Then stitch across the short curved seam at the hand/shoe end. Turn each piece to the right side and stuff with toy filling—be sure not to overfill the pieces. Now machine stitch or baste across the opening so the filling does not spill out.

3. Place one head and body piece flat on your counter with the right side facing you, then baste the top of each leg to the lower edge. Baste the top of each arm to the side of the body.

4. Fold the arms and legs inward, then place the front body and face on top. Baste the two pieces together, leaving a gap at the lower body edge to turn the doll shape to the right side. Turn through to the right side now, then stuff the body and head with toy filling. Carefully slipstitch the opening closed.

5. Stitch the side seams of the dress bodice together. Apply a narrow binding to the neck and armhole edges (see "binding" page 11), then join both shoulder seams. Stitch the center back skirt seam together and stitch a narrow double hem across the lower edge, then apply a strip of broderie anglaise lace trim. Dress Raggedy Ann and hand stitch the center back seam securely. Tie a gingham ribbon around her waist.

6. Using the picture as a guide, mark the eye, nose, and mouth position using a soft pencil or tailor's chalk. Use blue, white, and red embroidery thread to work the features. Hand stitch loops of chunky brown knitting yarn to the head to form Ann's hair and bangs. Make two long braids to complete her hairstyle, then finish with two pretty gingham ribbon bows.

Crib/stroller decoration

Folk-art heart and bird motifs combine to form a stylish crib or stroller decoration that has that special "homespun" feel. Why not hide a squeaker in one of the padded hearts as a surprise for curious little fingers to discover? This decoration uses just five shapes, but if you have time on your hands you could make lots more and extend it across a window in the nursery.

materials

- pencil and tracing paper
- sewing kit (see page 9) and sewing machine
- 4 in (10 cm) each of three toning small print cotton fabrics
- scraps of pale blue felt and pink felt for wings and tiny heart motif
- polyester toy filling
- squeakers (optional)
- tacky fabric adhesive

- blue embroidery thread
- 79-in (2-m) length x ½-in (1-cm) wide blue striped ribbon
- 79-in (2-m) length x ¼-in (6-mm) wide blue gingham ribbon

NOTE *Bird and heart templates include a ¼-in (6-mm) seam allowance. No allowance is needed for the wings and small heart.*

① Trace the heart and bird templates provided on page 89 onto tracing paper, then enlarge to the appropriate size as directed. Cut out two fabric pieces for each shape, plus one wing in felt for each bird and one small heart for the central shape.

② Place the fabric pieces together in pairs with the right sides facing. Stitch around the outer edge, taking a ¼-in (6-mm) seam allowance. Remember to leave a small gap in the stitching so that you can turn the shape through to the right side.

③ Turn each shape to the right side and stuff quite firmly with toy filling. You may at this stage insert a little squeaker in each one. Carefully slipstitch the opening closed.

◉ TEMPLATES P89

④ Use a spot of tacky fabric adhesive to secure the wings to each of the birds and a tiny heart to the central heart shape. When the glue is dry, stitch the wings in place with a small row of backstitches (see page 12), and the heart with one cross-stitch (see page 12).

⑤ Cut the wider ribbon in half and lay it out flat on your counter. Place the padded shapes on top, leaving about a 2-in (5-cm) gap between each one. Pin the shapes to the ribbon, then hand stitch securely in place, using double sewing thread and backstitches. Place the second strip of ribbon on top of the first just to hide the securing stitches.

⑥ To complete the decoration, cut the narrow gingham ribbon into six 8-in (20-cm) lengths. Tie each short length to the ribbon at each end and between the padded shapes—this secures the wider ribbon lengths and draws the shapes together a little. Secure each knot with a few overstitches, then tie each into a bow. Trim all ribbon ends into pretty points.

Cloth book

Small children and babies love to look at different shapes, colors, and patterns, even before they can read. A soft cloth book is the ideal starting point for young learners. This book is made entirely from cotton fabrics and pretty scraps rescued from the workbox and is completely washable—keep it in your changing bag to entertain your baby anytime, anywhere!

materials

- pencil and tracing paper
- sewing kit (see page 9) and sewing machine
- 8 in (20 cm) each red, yellow, green, blue, and lilac gingham fabrics
- 19½ in (50 cm) white cotton fabric
- scraps of plain cotton fabric to tone with gingham
- 12 in (30 cm) Wonder-Under™
- steam iron

NOTE *Templates include a ⁵⁄₈-in (1.5-cm) seam allowance. No allowance is needed for the shapes.*

TEMPLATES P86

① Trace the flower, fruit, and tree templates on page 86 onto tracing paper to make 12 shapes. Then enlarge to the appropriate size as directed. Follow the directions for machine appliqué on page 12, then cut out each piece in a different colored gingham or plain fabric. Leave enough gingham to edge the pages.

② Cut out six white cotton rectangles following the dimensions on the diagram, then fuse the shapes to each of the pages (see page 12). Each shape must be secured to the fabric "page" using a zigzag machine stitch.

③ Cut the remaining gingham fabric into 1½-in (4-cm) wide straight strips to use as binding for each page. Stitch a different colored gingham edge to each page, first along each short side and then across the top and bottom edges. Press the seams flat.

④ Place the pages right sides together in three pairs. Stitch together around the outside edge, taking a ⁵⁄₈-in (1.5-cm) seam allowance. Leave a small gap in the stitching at the lower edge so that you can turn the page to the right side.

⑤ Trim diagonally across the seam allowance at each corner, then turn each piece to the right side and press. Slipstitch the opening in the seam at the lower edge of the page.

⑥ Place the pages one on top of the other, choosing your favorite image to be the "front cover." Baste through all the layers at the center to secure. Now machine stitch the book together. Make sure to work three or four rows of machine stitching so that the pages will not come undone.

Clothes

Dress

What could be nicer for a baby girl than a pure white cotton piqué dress? This classic little number would be perfect for an afternoon stroll in the stroller or even at a party. The design is very simple to make and has a delicate daisy trim to accentuate the hems, neckline, and bodice seam.

materials

- pencil and tracing paper
- 39½ in (1 m) white cotton piqué
- 8 in (20 cm) lightweight iron-on interfacing
- steam iron
- sewing kit (see page 9) and sewing machine
- 3 small white buttons
- 118 in (3 m) daisy trim

NOTE *Templates have a ⅝-in (1.5-cm) seam allowance included and the skirt has a 2-in (5-cm) hem. The size is suitable for a 3- to 6-month-old baby.*

🌼 TEMPLATES P90

1 Trace the dress patterns provided on page 90 onto tracing paper, then enlarge to the appropriate size as directed. Cut out all the pieces from white cotton, then cut out the front and back neckline facings again from a lightweight iron-on interfacing. Fuse the interfacing to the wrong side of the facings using a steam iron.

2 Stitch the shoulder seams of the bodice and neckline facings together, then press the seams open. Apply the facing to the neckline with right sides together. Machine stitch along the center back edges and around the neckline. Trim the seam allowance down to about half and then clip into the curved neckline edges (see page 11).

3 Work a large gathering stitch between the marked dots on each sleeve head. Pull up the gathering stitches so that the sleeve fits into the armhole. Stitch each sleeve in place, then join the bodice side seam and sleeve seam in one. Fold and stitch a ½-in (1-cm) double hem around the lower edge of each sleeve.

4 Join the skirt seam from hemline to 2 in (5 cm) from top edge, then press the seam open. Fold and stitch a 1-in (2.5-cm) double hem around the lower edge. Now work a large gathering stitch around the top edge and gather up the skirt to fit the bodice seam. Pin and stitch the skirt to the bodice with right sides facing, keeping the gathers even all the way around.

5 Fold and press a ⅝-in (1.5-cm) turning along the center back bodice/skirt opening. Slipstitch the center back neck facing edges neatly to the turnings on the inside. Work three buttonholes on the center back overlap where indicated, then sew three buttons on the underlap to correspond.

6 Machine stitch the daisy trim to the stitching line of the skirt and sleeve hem, then around the neckline and along the bodice seam line.

Beach robe

Utilize a large bath sheet to make this cuddly and absorbent beach robe for your baby. All parents know how difficult it is to keep their baby still when they're trying to dry them after a dip in the bath or the sea. With this garment it's easy—just pop it over their heads and they can dry themselves as they run or crawl around. It's easily washable too, so all that sand and ice cream present no problem at all!

materials

- pencil and tracing paper
- one large patterned bath sheet
- sewing kit (see page 9) and sewing machine
- steam iron

NOTE *Templates include a ⅝-in (1.5-cm) seam allowance. Neaten all raw edges with a machine zigzag stitch to prevent fraying. The size is for a 6- to 9-month-old baby.*

TEMPLATES P93

1 Trace the patterns provided on page 93 onto tracing paper, then enlarge to the appropriate size as directed. Cut out all pattern pieces from the bath sheet as indicated. Remember to make use of the woven hems of the towel for the edge of the hood, lower edge of robe, and sleeve hems.

2 Join the front and back shoulder seams together with right sides facing. Neaten the seam allowances, then press the seam open.

3 Fold the hood piece in half with right sides together, then stitch the center back seam together. Stitch the neck seam to the neckline of the robe, taking care to overlap the front edges at the center front neckline point.

4 Fold and stitch a narrow hem along both side edges of the pocket piece, then baste a narrow hem along the upper and lower edges. Lay the robe out flat and pin the pocket in place just below the front neck in the center of the robe. Machine stitch the pocket in place along the upper and lower edges.

5 Pin the center of each sleeve head to the shoulder seam, then stitch the sleeves in place. Press both seams open.

6 Join the side and sleeve seams in one, then neaten the seam allowances with a machine zigzag stitch and press the seams open.

Cardigan

Cashmere and silk, what a luxurious combination—only the best for your baby! These natural fibers feel so soft and gentle against the skin that your baby will be extremely comfortable, and so smart too. This basic, T-shaped garment is very simply constructed, and finished with unusual velvet ribbon toggles.

materials

- pencil and tracing paper
- sewing kit (see page 9) and sewing machine
- a long cashmere and silk mix scarf
- 20 in (50 cm) striped silk fabric for the lining (this could also be a long head scarf)
- steam iron

- 39½-in (1-m) length of ½-in (1.5-cm) wide velvet ribbon in a toning shade for toggle fastenings

NOTE *Sleeve and the sides and armholes of the front and back templates include a ½-in (1-cm) seam allowance. The size is for a 3-month-old baby.*

⬤ TEMPLATES P91

① Trace the patterns provided on page 91 onto tracing paper, then enlarge to the appropriate size as directed. Cut out each piece from the knitted fabric and the striped silk lining fabric. Cut approximately 59 in (1.5 m) of 1½-in (4-cm) wide bias strips from the striped fabric for the bindings (see bias bindings on page 11).

② Start by stitching the shoulder seams of the cardigan together, then press the seams open. Stitch the sleeve to the armhole position matching the center sleeve head to the shoulder seam, then join the sleeve and side seams in one. Make up the cardigan lining in exactly the same way.

③ Press all seams open—you do not need to neaten the seam allowances. Turn the lining inside out, then place it inside the cardigan. Baste the wrist edges, lower hem, center front, and neckline edges together.

④ Cut 4 x 3-in (8-cm) lengths and 4 x 4-in (10-cm) lengths of velvet ribbon for the toggle and loop fastenings. Fold the four shorter pieces in half and baste the raw ends to the right center front edge, spacing evenly. The loop should lie flat and at this stage it will point toward the garment front.

⑤ For the toggle part of the fastening, simply fold the longer ribbon pieces in half and make a knot close to the folded end. Baste the raw edge to the left front edge to correspond with the loops on the other side.

⑥ Join the striped bias strips together to make one continuous strip and then apply the binding to the raw edges of the sleeves, the lower edge, and front/neckline edge (see page 11).

Felt bootees

Make the cutest pair of felt bootees as an unusual gift for a friend or relative with a new baby.

The two-tone pink and blue color scheme would suit a boy or a girl, and the tiny heart-

shape motif on the sole is a little surprise that will make the recipient smile.

● TEMPLATES P94

materials

- pencil and tracing paper
- sewing kit (see page 9) and sewing machine
- 2 large sheets of felt, one pink and one blue

- 39½ in (1 m) pink silk cord
- pinking shears

NOTE *Templates include a ¼-in (6-mm) seam allowance. The size is for a newborn baby.*

❶ Trace the patterns provided on page 94 onto tracing paper, then enlarge to the appropriate size as directed. Cut out the bootee pieces in pink and blue felt as indicated, plus a little pink heart motif for each bootee sole.

❷ Place a pink upper and a blue upper together and baste around the outside edges. Machine stitch the pieces together along the dotted line. Now trim the curved edge of the ankle cuff using pinking shears.

❸ Using a hole punch, carefully make three holes through both felt layers in the position indicated on the pattern. Make sure that the diameter is slightly larger than the diameter of your silk cord.

❹ Fold each upper in half with the pink layer on the inside. Stitch the center front seam together to the dot indicated on the template, taking a ¼-in (6-mm) seam allowance, then trim the seam allowance neatly using pinking shears.

❺ Position a heart shape on each sole and baste in place. Adjust your sewing machine to a small zigzag setting and carefully stitch around the outside edge of the shape to secure.

❻ Baste and machine stitch the sole to each bootee then pink the seam allowance neatly. Cut the pink silk cord in half and thread though the lacing holes on each bootee. Tie the ends in pretty bows. Trim all the long thread ends carefully, to a maximum length of ½ in (1 cm).

Hat

"If you want to get ahead, get a hat!" The greatest percentage of body heat is lost through the top of the head, and it is very important that a baby does not get cold on those chilly days out in the park. This little fleece number is made in a trice and the tassel on the top and the hand-worked running stitch detail add that special touch.

materials

- pencil and tracing paper
- sewing kit (see page 9) and sewing machine
- 12 in (30 cm) blue fleece fabric
- 12 in (30 cm) white fleece fabric
- pale blue and white embroidery thread

NOTE *Templates include a ⅝-in (1.5-cm) seam allowance. The size is for a 3-month-old baby.*

TEMPLATES P92

1 Trace the patterns provided on page 92 onto tracing paper, then enlarge to the appropriate size as directed. Cut out one piece in blue and one in white, placing the pattern piece to the fold, plus a tassel piece in each color.

2 Place the tassel pieces one on top of the other. Stitch together along the dotted line as indicated, then make parallel cuts from the outer edge toward the stitching line approximately ¼ in (6 mm) apart to form a fringe. Roll the tassel up tightly from the wider end and toward the shank, then secure the roll at the base with several handworked overstitches.

3 Begin with the white hat piece. Stitch the two short crown seams together, then baste the shank of the tassel to the point where the seams meet. Now join the longer center back/crown seam in one. All the seams should meet neatly at the top of the crown.

4 Make the blue lining in the same way, then place it inside the white hat piece, ensuring that the right sides are facing and that the lower edges match. Baste the lower seams together, then machine stitch. Remember to leave a small gap in the stitching so that you can turn the hat to the right side.

5 Turn the hat through to the right side and then slipstitch over the gap in the stitching to complete the basic construction.

6 Using a bodkin and blue and white embroidery thread, work a large but even running stitch around the lower edge of the hat (see page 12). This will help to keep the edge flat.

Baby's first mittens

Newborn babies have beautiful, tiny hands but often have extremely sharp fingernails, so they can easily scratch their delicate skin. Make these mittens from the softest fleece and line them with a pretty spotted lawn fabric to keep your baby warm and his or her skin protected.

materials

- pencil and tracing paper
- sewing kit (see page 9) and sewing machine
- 6 in (15 cm) ivory fleece fabric
- 6 in (15 cm) white and pink spotted cotton lawn fabric
- 12-in (30-cm) of ¼-in (6-mm) wide elastic
- 19½ in (50 cm) narrow satin ribbon in cream or pink

NOTE *Templates include a ¼-in (6-mm) seam allowance. The size is for a newborn baby.*

 TEMPLATE P92

① Trace the mitten pattern provided on page 92 onto tracing paper, then enlarge to the appropriate size as directed. Cut out two pieces in fleece and two in the spotted lawn fabric.

② Fold each piece in half with right sides together. Stitch the outer shaped edges together, taking a ¼-in (6-mm) seam allowance.

③ Turn both lining pieces to the right side. Now slip the spotted linings into the fleece mitten pieces. The right side of the lining should face the right side of the fleece mitten. Stitch the top edge together, leaving a small gap so you can turn the mitten through to the right side.

④ Turn the mittens through to the right side now, then slipstitch the small gap closed. Tuck the spotted lining down inside each fleece mitten, and baste close to the seam around the top edge.

⑤ This next part will be a little tricky, as the mittens are so small. Stitch a ½-in (1-cm) wide casing (see casings on page 10) about ¾ in (2 cm) from the top edge on both mittens. Unpick a few stitches in the seam between the casing stitching lines and thread a short piece of elastic through using a safety pin. Pull up the elastic a little, so that the wrist of each mitten is gathered but loose enough to let the baby's hand fit through. Stitch the ends of the elastic together.

⑥ Cut the ribbon in half and stitch the center of each piece to the casing on the underside of each mitten. Tie the ribbon in a pretty bow, then trim the ends to neat points. Trim all the long thread ends carefully, to a maximum length of ¼ in (1 cm).

Pants/dungarees

Perfect for napping, playing, or simply crawling around the floor, these cute dungarees are quick and easy to make—in fact, you could make several pairs to suit all seasons. The inside leg seam is fastened with Velcro™ for easy diaper changing—what could be better?

TEMPLATES P94

materials

- pencil and tracing paper
- sewing kit (see page 9) and sewing machine
- 31½ in (80 cm) blue star-patterned cotton fabric
- 12 in (30 cm) white cotton fabric for lining
- steam iron
- 10 small circular Velcro™ fasteners

NOTE *Templates have a ⅝-in (1.5-cm) seam allowance included. The size is for a 6- to 9-month-old baby.*

1 Trace the patterns provided on page 94 onto tracing paper, then enlarge to the appropriate size as directed. Cut out the pattern pieces from the blue star fabric as indicated, then cut the front and back bodice pieces again from plain white cotton lining fabric. Cut approximately 79 in (2 m) of 1½-in (4-cm) wide bias strips of blue fabric for the bindings (see bias binding on page 11).

2 Place the bodice pieces and the white linings together in pairs and baste together around the outside edges. Now join the front and back crotch seams together with right sides facing.

3 Work a large gathering stitch along the top edge of the front and back leg pieces. Pull up the gathering stitches a little to the leg pieces to fit the lower edge of the front and back bodice. Machine stitch in place.

4 Apply the binding to the armhole, neckline, and fastening tab edges of the front and back bodice. Fold and machine stitch a ½-in (1-cm) double hem across both ankle edges, then apply bias binding to each inside leg seam.

5 Place the front and back of the dungarees together with right sides facing, then join both side seams from ankle edge to the base of the fastening tab. Press the seams open and then turn to the right side. Topstitch the opening.

6 Separate the Velcro™ fasteners and stitch the loop part to the lining on the underlap and the hook part to the overlap of the inside leg opening, the side tabs, and the shoulder straps.

Fleece coat

Your baby will be so comfy and warm from head to toe in this full-length coat, she'll never want to take it off—whether it's an afternoon snooze or snuggling in the stroller while out walking. The toggles are made from fleece too, so there are no hard edges to disturb your baby's sleep.

materials

- pencil and tracing paper
- sewing kit (see page 9) and sewing machine
- 39½ in (1 m) each pale pink and dark pink fleece fabric

NOTE *Templates have a ⁵/₈-in (1.5-cm) seam allowance included. The size is for a 3- to 6-month-old baby.*

TEMPLATES P95

① Trace the patterns provided on page 95 onto tracing paper, then enlarge to the appropriate size as directed. Cut out all pattern pieces in pale pink and dark pink fleece fabric.

② Begin with the dark pink pieces. Join the shoulder seams together with right sides facing, then stitch each sleeve to the armhole position, matching the center sleeve head with the shoulder seam. Join the sleeve and side seam in one. Make the light pink fleece lining in exactly the same way.

③ Take the hood pieces and fold in half with right sides together. Join the center back seam first, then stitch across the short seam to give the hood a square shape. Stitch the lower edge of the hood to the neckline seam of the coat and lining.

④ Place the dark and light pink toggle pieces together in pairs and stitch together along the dotted line. Roll up the toggle from the wide end toward the shank. Secure the roll at the base with several hand stitches. Fold each loop piece in half, then topstitch close to the fold. Baste the toggles to the right front edge of the coat and the loops to the left.

⑤ Place the lining inside the outer coat with right sides together. Stitch the front edge and hood seam together, then turn the coat through to the right side. Topstitch the front edge and hood seam about ⁵/₈ in (1.5 cm) in from the edge. Slipstitch the hem of the coat and lining together around the wrist edge.

⑥ To complete the coat, stitch both layers together around the lower edge about 2 in (5 cm) up from the raw edge. Make a series of parallel cuts into the fleece fabric from the raw edge toward the stitching line to form a fringe.

Practical for parents

Padded hanger and drawstring bag

Padded hangers for special outfits look so much nicer and keep clothes looking special for longer. Choose a wooden, child-size hanger for this project—you could even recycle an old one that you already have. And why not make a tiny little drawstring bag to match the hanger, just to keep matching accessories, like socks and ribbons, safe.

materials

- pencil and tracing paper
- sewing kit (see page 9) and sewing machine
- 19½ in (50 cm) blue embroidered gingham fabric
- 8 in (20 cm) plain green fabric
- 12 in (30 cm) wadding
- wooden child-size coat hanger
- steam iron
- pale blue embroidery thread

NOTE *Bag measurements include a ⅝-in (1.5-cm) seam allowance.*

TEMPLATE P95

① Trace the pattern for the coat hanger provided on page 95 onto tracing paper, then enlarge to the appropriate size as directed. Cut out one hanger cover and one bag piece of 11 in x 4½ in (28 cm x 11 cm) from gingham fabric, and one bag piece of 11 in x 5 in (28 cm x 13 cm) from plain green fabric.. Cut 1½-in (4-cm) wide bias strips from the gingham to be used later for the hook covers, bows, and drawstrings.

② Cut a rectangle of wadding large enough to wrap around the hanger. Pierce a small hole in the center of the wadding and pass the hook through. Wrap the edges of the wadding snugly around the wooden hanger and baste securely in place.

③ For the hook cover, cut a 4-in (10-cm) length of bias strip from gingham fabric and fold it in half, then stitch across the short end and up the side edge. Turn the cover to the right side and slip it over the hook. Stitch the raw end of the hook cover to the wadding at the base of the hook.

④ Pierce a small hole through the center of the fabric hanger cover, then pass the hook through. Wrap the fabric around the padded hanger and fold in the raw edges at each end and along the lower edge. Slipstitch the folds together neatly.

⑤ Join both bag pieces together and press the seam open. Work a row of cross-stitches on the seam line using blue embroidery thread (see page 12). Fold the bag in half with right sides together, then stitch across the bottom edge and side edges. Fold a 1-in (2.5-cm) hem around the top edge, then stitch ⅝ in (1.5 cm) from the fold to form a casing. Unpick a few stitches in the seam between the stitching lines of the casing.

⑥ Cut two 10-in (25-cm) lengths of bias binding from the gingham. Fold each in half and stitch across both short ends. Then stitch across the long edge, leaving a small gap in the stitching at the center. Turn the strips to the right side through the gap to form the tie and the drawstring, then slipstitch the gap closed. Now stitch the tie to the base of the hook and then tie in a bow. Thread the drawstring through the casing at the top of the bag, then tie the ends in a knot.

Storage bucket

Storage with a difference! Any household containing a small baby quickly becomes overwhelmed with bottles, tubes, lotions and potions, powders, and other vital bits and pieces of baby toiletry. Use a galvanized bucket as an unusual storage item with a pretty drawstring bag inside. It's sturdy, waterproof, and stylish too, for use in the bathroom, garden, or even on the beach.

materials

- white primer
- paintbrush
- galvanized bucket
- green and pink spray paint or metal paint
- sewing kit (see page 9) and sewing machine
- 39½ in (1 m) pink gingham fabric
- 39½ in (1 m) green canvas
- eyelet kit
- steam iron

NOTE *Measurements include a ⅝-in (1.5-cm) seam allowance.*

① Apply a coat of white primer to the galvanized bucket and, when dry, apply the green and pink paint in wide bands as shown.

② Cut a circle from the pink gingham the size of the base of the bucket, then cut a rectangle from green canvas and pink gingham to fit the circumference of the top of the bucket and about twice the height. For the drawstring, cut a gingham strip 3 in x 39½ in (8 cm x 1 m). For the ties, cut two strips 6 in x 2 in (15 cm x 5 cm) from gingham fabric.

③ Indicate a 1½-in (4-cm) wide casing about 3 in (8 cm) down from the top edge of the green canvas piece, using tailor's chalk. Mark two eyelet positions at the center of the casing, then insert as per kit directions. Fold both the canvas and lining pieces in half and stitch the side seams together. Press the seams flat.

④ Place the bag and lining together with right sides facing. Stitch together along to the upper edge. Turn to the right side and tuck the lining inside the bag. Press the seam flat, then topstitch close to the upper edge. Stitch a 1½-in (4-cm) wide casing where indicated, making sure that the eyelets are correctly positioned.

⑤ Pin the bag and lining layers together along the lower raw edge, then work a large gathering stitch close to the edge. Pull up the gathering stitches so that the bag fits the circular fabric base. Stitch the bag to the base, placing the right side of the base to the inside of the bag, so the raw edge will not be seen inside the bag.

⑥ For the ties and drawstring, fold the long and short strips in half with right sides facing, then stitch across each short end and along the side seam leaving a gap at the center. Turn the strips to the right side and slipstitch over the gaps, then press the strips. Stitch one short tie to each side of the bucket, and thread the long drawstring through the casing. Place the bag inside the bucket and secure the ties to the handle on each side.

Changing bag

Every new parent is surprised by how much "stuff" they need to carry around with them when they have a small baby to look after. This voluminous canvas bag is large enough to hold just about everything you could possibly need—and more! It has long carry handles and three extra pockets on the outside for small items. What's more, the bag folds completely flat for easy storage when not in use.

materials

- pencil and paper
- scissors
- 39½ in (1 m) turquoise canvas cotton fabric
- 39½ in (1 m) print cotton fabric for lining
- sewing kit (see page 9) and sewing machine
- steam iron
- scrap Velcro™ for tab

NOTE *Templates include a ⅝-in (1.5-cm) seam allowance.*

TEMPLATES P94

1 Make paper patterns for the bag, pocket, straps, and tabs following the diagrams given on page 94. Cut out two bag pieces, one pocket, and two straps from the canvas and the print fabric, plus one print fabric tab.

2 Place the pocket and lining pieces together with right sides facing, then stitch across the top edge. Press the seam open, then refold the pocket so the wrong sides are facing. Repress the top seam, then topstitch close to the edge (see topstitching on page 11). Place the pocket onto the bag front, matching the lower stepped edges. Stitch vertical pocket divisions where indicated on the pattern.

3 Place the two bag pieces together with right sides facing. Stitch the side seams together, then stitch the seam that runs across the lower edge. Pin the side seams to the lower seam, then stitch the edges together. This forms the square-shaped base of the bag.

4 Make the lining up in exactly the same way, but leave a gap in the seam that runs along the base so you can turn the bag to the right side. Place the lining inside the bag with right sides facing. Stitch both layers together around the top edge. Now turn the bag and lining to the right side through the gap in the lower lining seam. Slipstitch the gap closed.

5 Tuck the lining down inside the bag and press the top seam neatly. Topstitch close to the fold along the top edge. Fold the tab piece in half with right sides together, then stitch down the side and across one short end. Turn it through to the right side and press, then stitch a small piece of Velcro™ to the underside at one end. Stitch the tab to the bag just inside the top of the middle pocket, then stitch on a corresponding Velcro™ fastening to outside of the pocket under the tab.

6 Place both canvas straps and the lining pieces together with right sides facing, then stitch together down both long sides. Turn the straps to the right side and topstitch close to both side edges. Fold a ⅝-in (1.5-cm) hem across the short ends, then pin and machine stitch the straps in place on the bag as shown in the picture.

Laundry bag

It is truly amazing how much laundry your tiny little bundle can generate in just a day! Our laundry bag, with pretty three-dimensional daisies, has a huge capacity and drawstring ties for hanging on a hook inside the nursery door. It's made entirely from pure cotton, so you can pop the bag into the wash whenever it's necessary.

materials

- pencil, paper, and tracing paper
- sewing kit (see page 9) and sewing machine
- 19½ in (50 cm) pink chambray fabric
- 10 in (25 cm) blue chambray fabric
- 27½ in (70 cm) white cotton fabric
- 12 in (30 cm) blue gingham fabric
- steam iron
- handful of polyester toy filling

NOTE *Bag templates include a ⁵⁄₈-in (1.5-cm) seam allowance. Flower template includes a ¼-in (6-mm) seam allowance.*

TEMPLATE P87

❶ Make paper patterns for the bag following the diagrams provided on page 87, then trace the daisy template onto tracing paper and enlarge to the appropriate size as directed. Cut out the bag pieces from pink and blue chambray, the lining from white cotton, and the daisy shapes from white cotton and blue gingham. Cut approximately 60 in (1.5 m) of 1½-in (4-cm) wide bias strips, and 60 in (1.5 m) of 1½-in (4-cm) wide straight strips from blue gingham for the binding and the drawstring.

❷ Place the white daisy shapes together in three pairs. Stitch together around the outside edge, taking a ¼-in (6-mm) seam allowance, remembering to leave a small gap in the stitching. Snip into the seam allowance at the corners and clip the curved edges (see page 11). Now turn the shapes through to the right side. Slipstitch the gap closed, then press the shapes flat.

❸ Stitch together the pink and blue chambray pieces and press the seam open. Baste the daisy shapes in place side by side along the seam on the front half of the bag. Place the gingham circles in the center of each flower. Tuck a small amount of toy filling under each circle, then tuck in the raw outside edge, baste in place, and machine stitch to the bag.

❹ Stitch the side and lower seams of the bag and lining together, then place the lining inside the bag with the wrong sides facing. Baste the top edges together, then apply the blue gingham binding to cover the raw edge (see page 11).

❺ Now fold the long raw edges of the straight gingham strip to the center and then fold in half again. Tuck in the raw edges at each short end and then machine stitch close to the edge to make the drawstring.

❻ Stitch a ¾-in (2-cm) wide casing (see page 10) approximately 4 in (10 cm) down from the top edge. Unpick a few stitches in the seam that lies between the stitching lines of the casing, and then thread the drawstring through using a safety pin. Tie the drawstring in a bow or knot the ends together.

Changing mat

Your baby needs changing regularly—whether you're at home or on the move. Carry this pretty roll-up changing mat over your shoulder when you and your baby are out and about. There's a pretty floral cotton print on one side and polka dot wipe clean oilcloth on the other.

materials

- pencil and paper
- small plate or saucer
- sewing kit (see page 9) and sewing machine
- 23½ in (60 cm) blue spotted oilcloth
- 31½ in (80 cm) floral print cotton fabric to tone with the oilcloth
- steam iron

1 Make a paper rectangular pattern measuring 31½ in x 19¾ in (80 cm x 50 cm). Use a small plate or saucer as a template to round off each corner. Cut out one piece in oilcloth and one in cotton fabric.

2 Cut two 3-in x 31½-in (9-cm x 80-cm) strips of the floral cotton fabric for the carry handle and tie, then cut about 118 in (3 m) of 1½-in (4-cm) wide bias strips from the cotton for the binding.

3 Place the cotton and oilcloth pieces together with wrong sides facing. Baste together around the outside edge. Take the carry handle strip and fold it in half lengthwise. Stitch the long edges together, then turn it through to the right side and press. Baste the raw ends of the handle to the long sides of the mat on the cotton side about 6 in (15 cm) down from one end so that it stretches across the mat.

4 Join the floral bias strips together to form one continuous length, then apply the binding to the outside edge of the mat (see page 11).

5 Take the remaining tie strip and fold it in half lengthwise. Stitch across the short ends and down the long edge, leaving a small gap in the stitching at the center so that you can turn the tie to the right side. Trim diagonally across the seam allowances at each corner (see page 11), then turn the strip to the right side and press flat.

6 Slipstitch the gap closed, then fold the strip in half. Machine stitch the halfway point of the tie to the mat on the floral side at the center of the short end, nearest the carry handle.

Diaper dispenser

How many diapers will you use during your baby's early years, you may wonder? Although an absolutely essential part of your babycare equipment, the plastic bag packaging is not really very pretty, is it? Why not make a little dispenser to hold your disposable diapers, or even terry nappies if folded up neatly? Think "duffel bag" when you make this—it's simpler than it looks.

materials

- pencil and paper
- sewing kit (see page 9) and sewing machine
- 39½ in (1 m) pink spotted fabric
- eyelet kit
- steam iron
- 39½ in (1 m) white cord
- 2 circular Velcro™ fasteners
- thick card
- fabric adhesive

NOTE *Templates include a ⁵/₈-in (1.5-cm) seam allowance. Material allowances are based on a pack of newborn baby diapers.*

TEMPLATES P93

1 Make a paper pattern following the diagrams provided on page 93. Cut out one bag piece, one base, and a flap from the spotted fabric. Cut a rectangle of fabric about 2 in (5 cm) larger than the base all round to cover the base stiffener. Cut 19½ in (50 cm) of 1½-in (4-cm) wide bias strip for the binding.

2 Apply the bias binding to the curved edge of the semicircular opening (see page 11). Now fold a 4-in (10-cm) wide hem along the top edge. Stitch a 1½-in (4-cm) wide casing about 1 in (2.5 cm) from the top edge (see page 10). Mark eight evenly spaced eyelet hole positions along the casing and insert each one following the kit directions.

3 Fold the flap in half with right sides together, then stitch across both short sides. Turn to the right side and press, then topstitch close to three edges, leaving the raw edge free. Baste the two lower corners of the flap to the base of the semicircular opening on both sides.

4 Stitch the rectangular base to the lower edge of the dispenser bag with right sides facing, taking care to snip into the seam allowance at each corner so that the fabric lies flat. Now turn the bag to the right side.

5 Cut a strip of fabric about 4 in x 2 in (10 cm x 5 cm). Fold the long raw edges to the center, then fold in half again. Fold the short ends to the center and overlap slightly. Machine stitch through all the layers at the center to form a fabric "stay" for the drawstring. Thread the cord drawstring through the eyelets and through the fabric stay. Tie the ends of the cord together in a knot and tuck inside the bag out of sight.

6 Separate the two Velcro™ fasteners, then stitch the hook part to each corner of the flap and the loop part to the dispenser in a corresponding position. Wrap the remaining rectangle of fabric around a stiff piece of card cut to fit the dispenser base. Glue the edges of the fabric to the card on the underside. When the glue is dry, pop the stiffener into the base.

Bib

Let's face it, when it comes to feeding time, babies don't really care where the food goes—keeping clothes clean is just not a priority! Protect garments with a good old-fashioned bib. Our two pretty bibs are completely washable, and the acrylic paint is permanent when dry, so the cute Scottie-dog motifs won't fade or run in the washing machine.

materials

- pencil and tracing paper
- sewing kit (see page 9)
- 15½ in (40 cm) white cotton fabric
- 12 in (30 cm) red gingham fabric
- 12 in (30 cm) black gingham fabric
- sheet of thick card
- painter's tape
- stencil acetate
- spray stencil adhesive
- red and black acrylic paint
- saucer or palette
- stencil brush
- small artist's paintbrush
- 2 circular Velcro™ fastenings

⬤ TEMPLATES P89

① Trace the patterns for the bib shape and the Scottie stencil provided on page 89 onto tracing paper, then enlarge to the appropriate size as directed. Cut two bib pieces from white cotton (you can use a double layer if the cotton is quite fine), then cut about 39½ in (1 m) of 1½-in (4-cm) wide bias binding from both the red and black gingham fabric.

② Fix the tracing outline to a piece of thick card using tabs of painter's tape, and tape the acetate sheet on top. Carefully cut out the stencil using a scalpel (see stenciling, page 13).

③ Lightly coat the back of the stencil with adhesive spray, then place in position on the bib. Pour some red paint onto a saucer or palette, then take up a little on the stencil brush. Dab off excess paint on a spare sheet of paper, then apply the paint through the stencil (see page 13). Do likewise on the other bib, but use black paint.

④ When the stencil work is dry, use a small artist's brush to paint in the details. Give the red Scotties a black collar and eyes, and the black Scotties red collars and eyes. You could alternate red and black Scotties on the same bib if you want to be a little more creative.

⑤ Join the red bias strips together to make one continuous length and the black bias strips together to make a second, then apply the red binding to the bib with black Scotties, and the black binding to the bib with the red Scotties.

⑥ Separate both Velcro™ fasteners and then, on each bib, stitch the loop part to the bib underlap at the neckline and the hook part to the overlap.

Hooded towel and wash mitt

A classic babycare item—once you've used one of these, you will never look back. Bathtime with a new baby is always fun for parents and little ones alike, but drying a wet wriggling baby afterward can be easier said than done! Swaddle your baby in this fluffy hooded towel after bathing, and he or she will soon be dry. There is a matching wash mitt too, for having fun with bubbles and getting clean.

materials

- large white bath sheet
- sewing kit (see page 9) and sewing machine
- 12 in (30 cm) multi-colored, striped cotton fabric
- small saucer

1 Lay the bath sheet out flat and cut off a strip along one short end to make one large square. Cut approximately 158 in (4 m) of 1½-in (4-cm) wide bias strips from the striped cotton fabric.

2 From the towel offcut, cut a right-angle triangle measuring about 14 in (36 cm) along the right-angled sides. Make sure that the diagonal edge runs along the woven towel edge so that you won't have to stitch a hem.

3 Place the triangle across one corner of the towel square and baste the edges in place. Use a small saucer as a template to round off each corner of the towel.

4 Make a hanging loop from a short strip of striped fabric folded in half twice lengthwise. Fold the strip in half again, then baste both raw ends to the top of the hood part of the towel.

5 Join the bias strips together to make a continuous length. Now apply the binding to the outer edge of the towel (see page 11).

6 For the wash mitt, simply cut out a rectangle of toweling measuring 8 in x 12 in (20 cm x 30 cm). Fold in half matching the shortest edges. Stitch across the lower edge and up the side seam. Make a small loop from a scrap of striped fabric and baste it to the top edge. Turn the mitt to the right side, then apply bias binding to the top raw edge (see page 11).

Templates

The templates supplied here list how much you need to enlarge them by to make the projects in the book. You can make the projects at different sizes, but you should keep the proportions the same.

CLOTH BOOK (ENLARGE BY 200%)

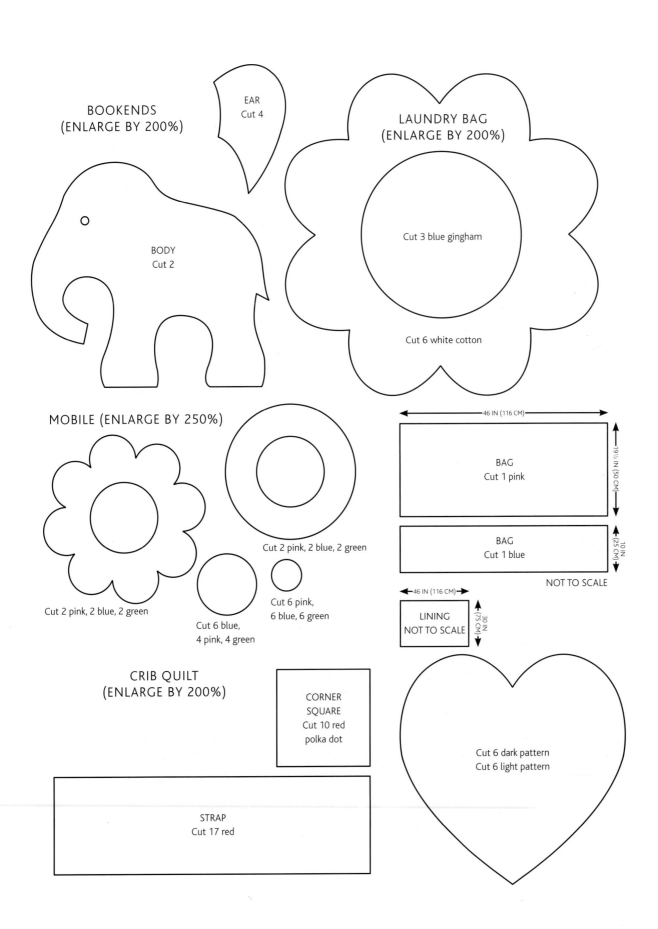

BOOKENDS
(ENLARGE BY 200%)

EAR
Cut 4

BODY
Cut 2

LAUNDRY BAG
(ENLARGE BY 200%)

Cut 3 blue gingham

Cut 6 white cotton

MOBILE (ENLARGE BY 250%)

Cut 2 pink, 2 blue, 2 green

Cut 2 pink, 2 blue, 2 green

Cut 6 pink,
6 blue, 6 green

Cut 6 blue,
4 pink, 4 green

←— 46 IN (116 CM) —→

BAG
Cut 1 pink

19½ IN (50 CM)

BAG
Cut 1 blue

10 IN (25 CM)

NOT TO SCALE

←— 46 IN (116 CM) —→

LINING
NOT TO SCALE

30 IN (75 CM)

CRIB QUILT
(ENLARGE BY 200%)

CORNER
SQUARE
Cut 10 red
polka dot

Cut 6 dark pattern
Cut 6 light pattern

STRAP
Cut 17 red

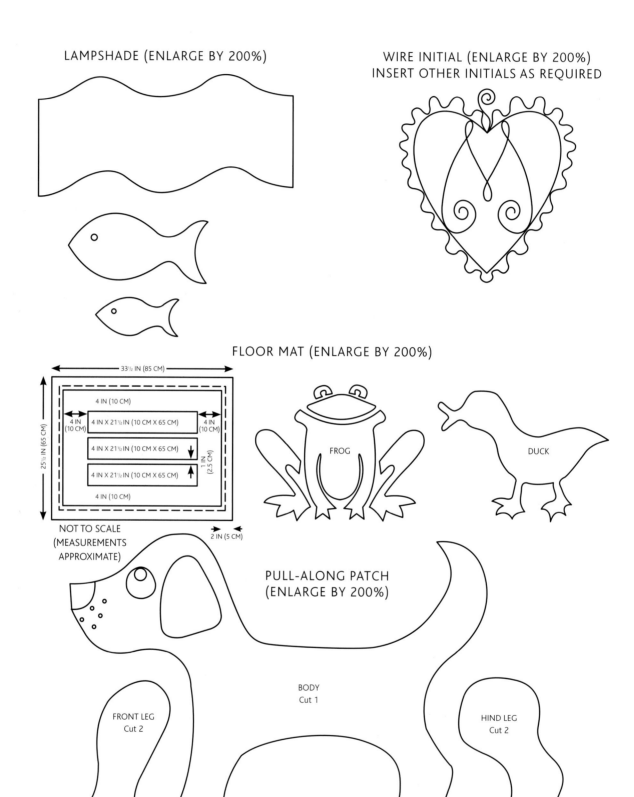

LAMPSHADE (ENLARGE BY 200%)

WIRE INITIAL (ENLARGE BY 200%)
INSERT OTHER INITIALS AS REQUIRED

FLOOR MAT (ENLARGE BY 200%)

33½ IN (85 CM)

4 IN (10 CM)

4 IN
(10 CM)

4 IN X 21½ IN (10 CM X 65 CM)

4 IN
(10 CM)

25½ IN (65 CM)

4 IN X 21½ IN (10 CM X 65 CM)

1 IN
(2.5 CM)

4 IN X 21½ IN (10 CM X 65 CM)

4 IN (10 CM)

NOT TO SCALE
(MEASUREMENTS
APPROXIMATE)

2 IN (5 CM)

FROG

DUCK

PULL-ALONG PATCH
(ENLARGE BY 200%)

FRONT LEG
Cut 2

BODY
Cut 1

HIND LEG
Cut 2

CRIB/STROLLER DECORATION
(ENLARGE BY 200%)

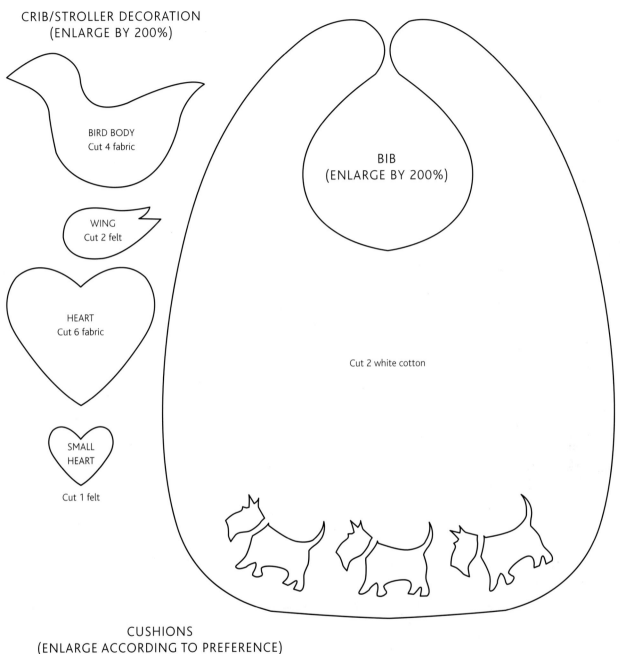

BIRD BODY
Cut 4 fabric

WING
Cut 2 felt

HEART
Cut 6 fabric

SMALL
HEART

Cut 1 felt

BIB
(ENLARGE BY 200%)

Cut 2 white cotton

CUSHIONS
(ENLARGE ACCORDING TO PREFERENCE)

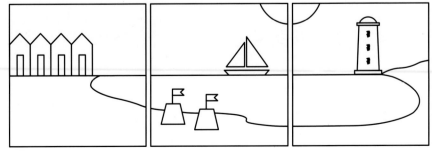

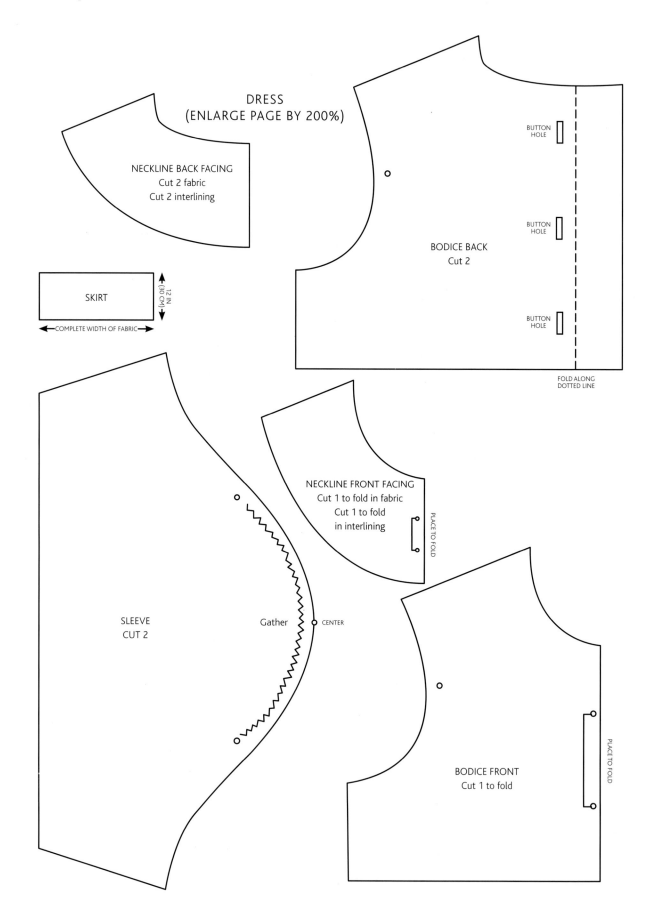

DRESS
(ENLARGE PAGE BY 200%)

NECKLINE BACK FACING
Cut 2 fabric
Cut 2 interlining

SKIRT

12 IN
(30 CM)

←COMPLETE WIDTH OF FABRIC→

BUTTON
HOLE

BUTTON
HOLE

BODICE BACK
Cut 2

BUTTON
HOLE

FOLD ALONG
DOTTED LINE

NECKLINE FRONT FACING
Cut 1 to fold in fabric
Cut 1 to fold
in interlining

PLACE TO FOLD

SLEEVE
CUT 2

Gather

CENTER

BODICE FRONT
Cut 1 to fold

PLACE TO FOLD

CARDIGAN
(ENLARGE PAGE BY 200%)

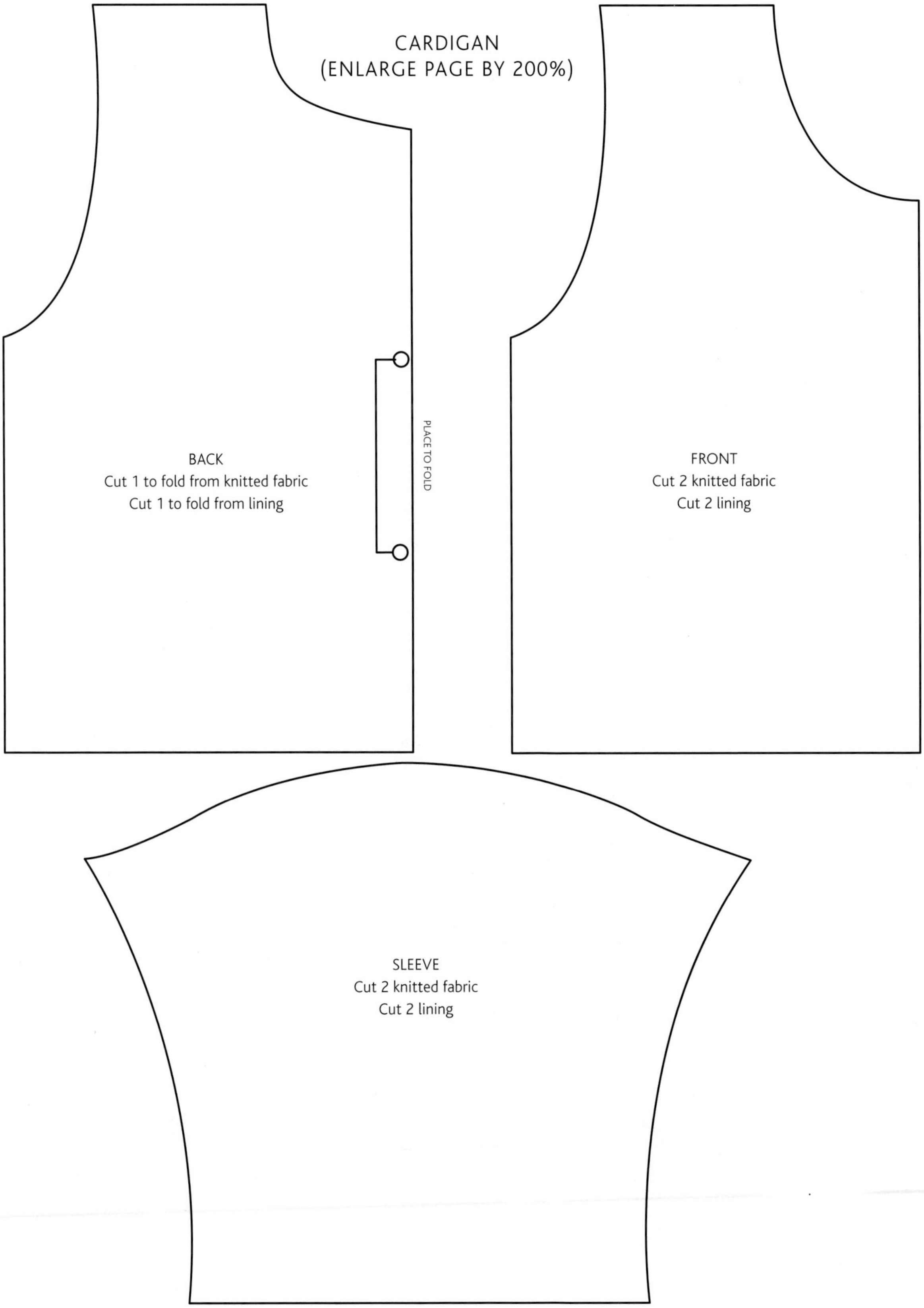

BACK
Cut 1 to fold from knitted fabric
Cut 1 to fold from lining

PLACE TO FOLD

FRONT
Cut 2 knitted fabric
Cut 2 lining

SLEEVE
Cut 2 knitted fabric
Cut 2 lining

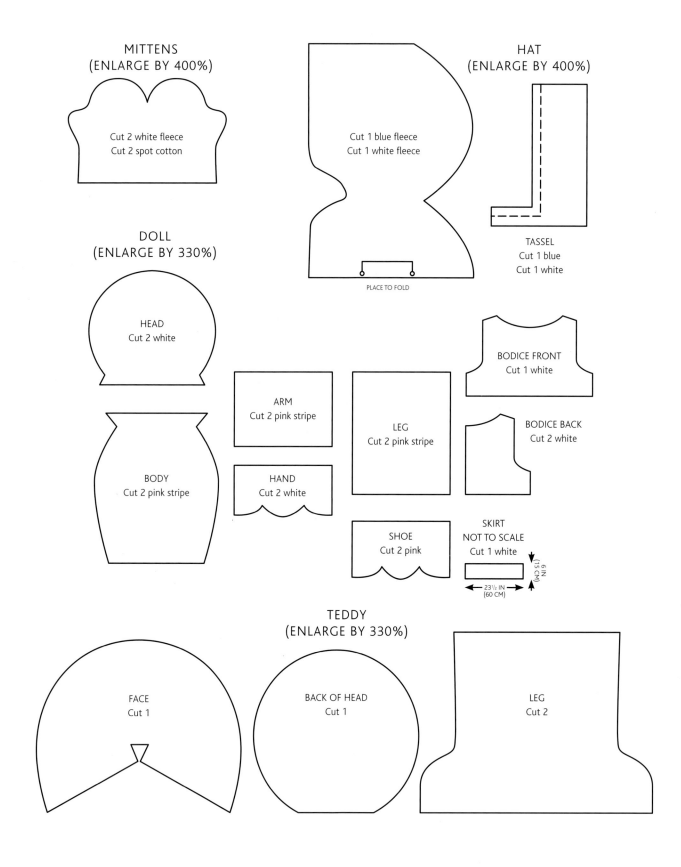

MITTENS
(ENLARGE BY 400%)

Cut 2 white fleece
Cut 2 spot cotton

HAT
(ENLARGE BY 400%)

Cut 1 blue fleece
Cut 1 white fleece

PLACE TO FOLD

TASSEL
Cut 1 blue
Cut 1 white

DOLL
(ENLARGE BY 330%)

HEAD
Cut 2 white

ARM
Cut 2 pink stripe

LEG
Cut 2 pink stripe

BODICE FRONT
Cut 1 white

BODICE BACK
Cut 2 white

BODY
Cut 2 pink stripe

HAND
Cut 2 white

SHOE
Cut 2 pink

SKIRT
NOT TO SCALE
Cut 1 white

6 IN
(15 CM)

23½ IN
(60 CM)

TEDDY
(ENLARGE BY 330%)

FACE
Cut 1

BACK OF HEAD
Cut 1

LEG
Cut 2

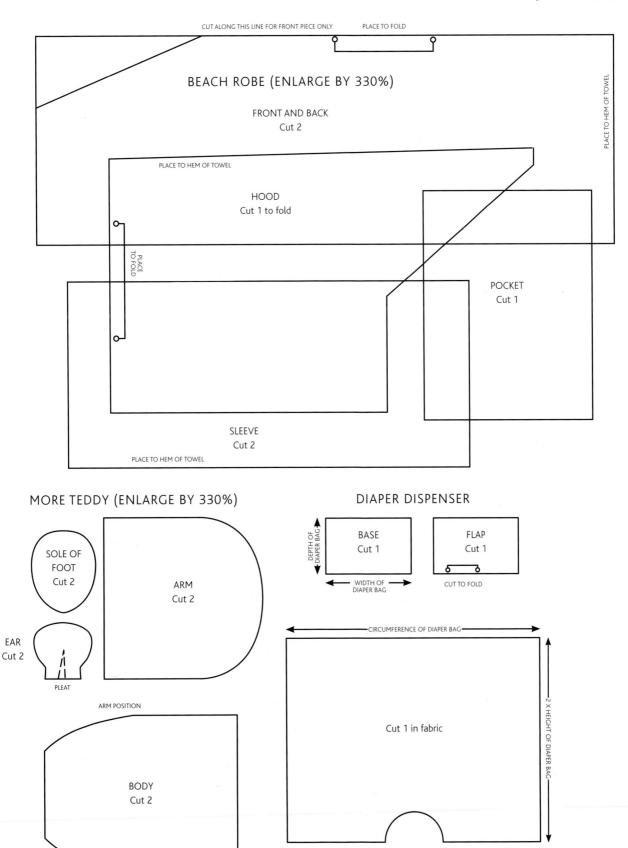

CUT ALONG THIS LINE FOR FRONT PIECE ONLY   PLACE TO FOLD

BEACH ROBE (ENLARGE BY 330%)

FRONT AND BACK
Cut 2

PLACE TO HEM OF TOWEL

PLACE TO HEM OF TOWEL

HOOD
Cut 1 to fold

PLACE TO FOLD

POCKET
Cut 1

SLEEVE
Cut 2

PLACE TO HEM OF TOWEL

MORE TEDDY (ENLARGE BY 330%)

SOLE OF
FOOT
Cut 2

ARM
Cut 2

EAR
Cut 2

PLEAT

ARM POSITION

BODY
Cut 2

ARM POSITION

DIAPER DISPENSER

DEPTH OF DIAPER BAG

BASE
Cut 1

FLAP
Cut 1

WIDTH OF
DIAPER BAG

CUT TO FOLD

CIRCUMFERENCE OF DIAPER BAG

2 X HEIGHT OF DIAPER BAG

Cut 1 in fabric

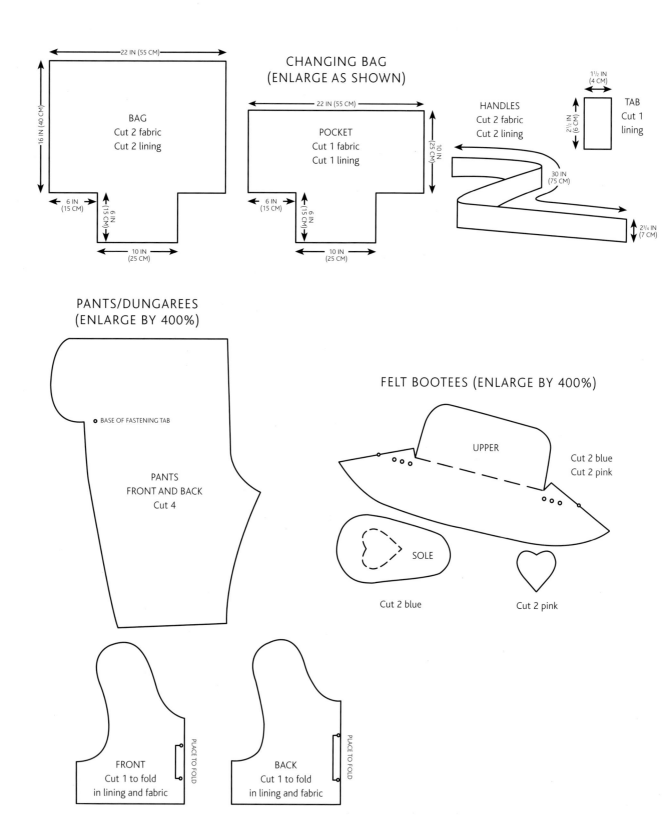

CHANGING BAG
(ENLARGE AS SHOWN)

22 IN (55 CM)

16 IN (40 CM)

BAG
Cut 2 fabric
Cut 2 lining

6 IN
(15 CM)

6 IN
(15 CM)

10 IN
(25 CM)

22 IN (55 CM)

POCKET
Cut 1 fabric
Cut 1 lining

10 IN
(25 CM)

6 IN
(15 CM)

6 IN
(15 CM)

10 IN
(25 CM)

HANDLES
Cut 2 fabric
Cut 2 lining

30 IN
(75 CM)

2³/₄ IN
(7 CM)

1¹/₂ IN
(4 CM)

2¹/₂ IN
(6 CM)

TAB
Cut 1
lining

PANTS/DUNGAREES
(ENLARGE BY 400%)

BASE OF FASTENING TAB

PANTS
FRONT AND BACK
Cut 4

FELT BOOTEES (ENLARGE BY 400%)

UPPER

Cut 2 blue
Cut 2 pink

SOLE

Cut 2 blue

Cut 2 pink

FRONT
Cut 1 to fold
in lining and fabric

PLACE TO FOLD

BACK
Cut 1 to fold
in lining and fabric

PLACE TO FOLD

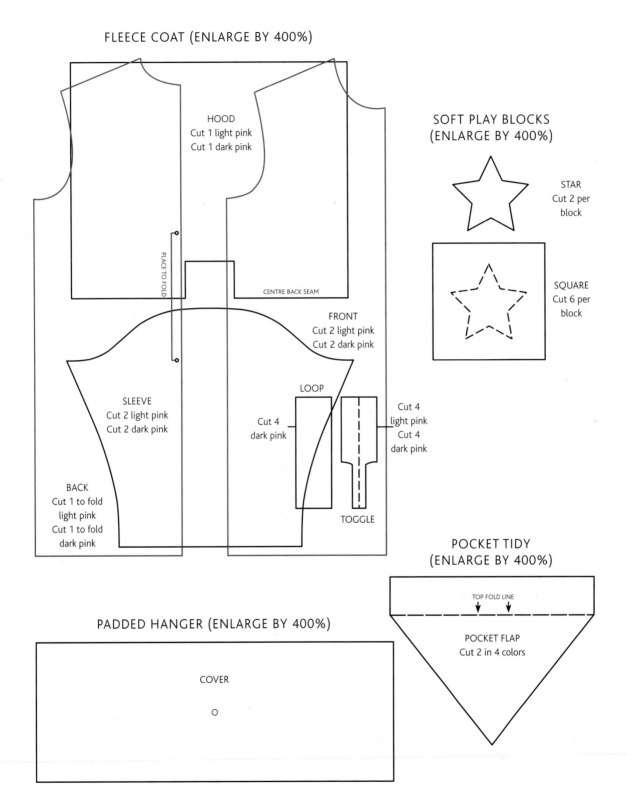

FLEECE COAT (ENLARGE BY 400%)

HOOD
Cut 1 light pink
Cut 1 dark pink

PLACE TO FOLD

CENTRE BACK SEAM

FRONT
Cut 2 light pink
Cut 2 dark pink

SLEEVE
Cut 2 light pink
Cut 2 dark pink

LOOP
Cut 4
dark pink

Cut 4
light pink
Cut 4
dark pink

TOGGLE

BACK
Cut 1 to fold
light pink
Cut 1 to fold
dark pink

SOFT PLAY BLOCKS
(ENLARGE BY 400%)

STAR
Cut 2 per
block

SQUARE
Cut 6 per
block

PADDED HANGER (ENLARGE BY 400%)

COVER

O

POCKET TIDY
(ENLARGE BY 400%)

TOP FOLD LINE

POCKET FLAP
Cut 2 in 4 colors

Index